Integrating Art and Language Arts through Children's Literature

Integrating Art and Language Arts through Children's Literature

Debi Englebaugh

2003
Teacher Ideas Press
Libraries Unlimited
A Division of Greenwood Publishing Group, Inc.
Westpost, Connecticut

To Robert, Taylor, and Morgan

TEACHER IDEAS PRESS
Libraries Unlimited
A Division of Greenwood Publishing Group, Inc.
88 Post Road West
Westport, CT 06881
1-800-225-5800
www.lu.com/tips

ISBN 1-56308-958-0

Contents

Part 2: Lessons

Introduction

    Integrating Art and Language Arts through Children's Literature is a resource book that takes a variety of children's literature and provides classroom teachers with creative lessons. The lessons can be adjusted to meet the needs of any elementary class.

    The book is divided into two sections. The first section describes art techniques that can be adapted to favorite children's books. There are so many books suitable for use in the classroom that it would be impossible to provide a lesson for every book. Many books can be easily adapted to these art techniques.

    The second section lists more than 140 different books with lessons, covering a range of topics. The books are organized alphabetically by title. Most of the books have been published in the past 10 years and are available in bookstores and online. Some of the lessons explore the technique the artist used when creating the illustrations, and some of the lessons deal with the book's theme or a single subject in the book. Every lesson is a link to language arts because a children's book is the source. Many of the lessons also provide a specific language arts lesson that goes along with the art lesson. For example, the handmade book lessons provide instructions for making the handmade book as well as ideas to motivate writing.

    A brief description about each book is provided, as well as a basic supply list and simple instructions. The book also provides Web links. Many of the authors have Web pages that provide facts about the author and information about additional books.

Part 1

Art Techniques

Artistamps

Artistamps are fake postage stamps created by artists. They are used next to legal postage stamps and have the appearance of real stamps. Artistamps are a type of mail art that were created in the 1960s. Mail art was started by artists who didn't believe art should be limited to gallery and museum walls. The aim of mail art is to create artwork that can be exchanged. Mail artists use a variety of art forms including collage, rubber stamps, postcards, stickers, and faux postage stamps.

Supplies

Photocopy of the stamp pattern
Pencil
Colored pencils
Thumbtacks

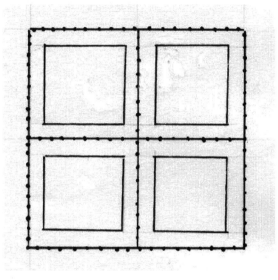

Instructions

1. Make copies of the stamp pattern. Have several examples of legal postage stamps including cancelled stamps on delivered mail and newly purchased blocks of stamps.

2. Use pencil and colored pencils to draw a design on the group of stamps. Once the drawing is complete, add the perforations using a thumbtack. Place the finished artistamp on an envelope next to a real stamp.

Web Sites

Junior Philatelists of America. URL: http://www.jpastamps.org/

United States Postal Service. URL: http://www.usps.gov/

United States Stamp Society. URL: http://www.usstamps.org/

American Philatelic Society Kids Page. URL: http://www.stamps.org/kids/

Assemblage

Assemblage is the art of placing three-dimensional objects in an arrangement. A variety of backgrounds can be used as a base to attach the elements of the assemblage. Backgrounds can include cardboard, wood, and picture frames. Wrapping paper, magazine pictures, and labels from canned food and cereal boxes can also be used for the background. Three-dimensional objects such as boxes, bottles, and vases are attached to the background.

Supplies

Found objects
Background papers
Staples
Glue
Pins
Thumbtacks

Instructions

1. Use a variety of small objects such as small plastic toys from fast-food restaurants, toys from bubble gum–type machines, small pieces from old board games, old kitchen gadgets, sewing items, play jewelry, and old art supplies.

2. Attach the objects to the background. The lighter objects can be glued; the heavier objects will need to be secured with tacks, staples, or pins.

Batik

Batik is the technique of creating an image on fabric by coating areas with wax to resist absorbing the dye or paint. The area that is coated with wax will remain the original color when it comes in contact with paint or dye. Then the wax is removed with heat.

Supplies

Cloth
Melted wax
Brushes
Pencils
Hot iron
Paper towels
Newspaper
Paint or dye

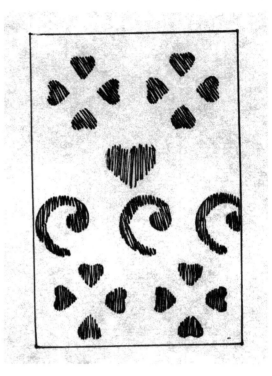

Instructions

1. Draw a design on the cloth using pencil.

2. Brush melted wax onto the areas that you want to remain the color of the cloth.

3. Coat the surface of the cloth with paint or dye. The color will not absorb where the wax has been applied. Rinse carefully under running water.

4. Lay flat to dry. Once the cloth is dry, iron in between sheets of newspaper and paper towels to remove the wax.

Book Covers

This section is provided to accompany the lessons for handmade books. A variety of ideas are provided for making book covers. A book's cover can be as simple as a solid color paper with hand-printed words or the entire background can be covered with paint using a technique such as paste paper, plastic-wrap backgrounds, or Japanese Suminagashi. An alternative to decorating the entire surface is to decorate a small shape that can be attached to the cover paper. Any of the following techniques can be used to decorate the cover:

Bubble Paper

Collage

Crayon and Sandpaper Print on Paper

Japanese Suminagashi

Monoprinting

Paper Mosaics

Paste Paper

Plastic-Wrap Backgrounds

Photocopy Art, Prints

Prints with Fruits and Vegetables on Paper

Recycled Foam Tray Prints

Rubber Stamping

Stencils

Watercolor and Salt Design

Instructions

1. Decide if the entire cover is going to be decorated, just the front, or if an additional shape is to be added to the front.

2. Select the technique you would like to use. If the entire paper is to be decorated or the entire front cover, then it must be done before the book is constructed. If a small shape is to be added, this can be the last step in constructing the book.

Book with Accordion Pages

An accordion book is made using a fan fold so the pages of the book are continuous. A cover can be made from cover stock or oak tag. Pages can be joined from the back using tape.

Supplies

One sheet of 8-1/2" x 11" paper cut into two 4" x 11" pieces
Two pieces of 4-1/4" x 3" cardboard or poster board
Glue sticks
Clear tape

Instructions

1. Fold each sheet of paper in half.
2. Fold the sheets again in the opposite direction.
3. Tape the sheets together.
4. Attach the cover.

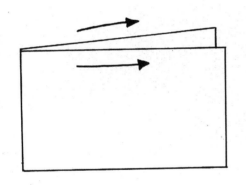
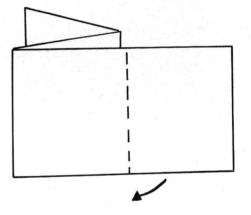
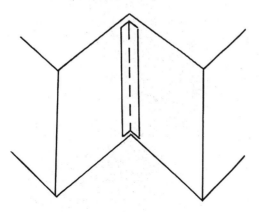
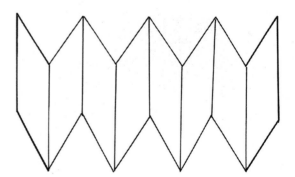

Book with Fan-Style Binding

Sheets of paper can be bound together in a book using a sheet of paper that has been accordion pleated. This design can be adapted to any size book; the instructions are provided for a 5-1/2" x 8-1/2" book.

Supplies

Six sheets of paper 5-1/2" x 8-1/2"

Two sheets of cover stock 5-1/2" x 8-1/2"

One sheet of paper 8-1/2" x11"

Glue stick

Instructions

1. Fold the 8-1/2" x 11" paper into an accordion fan.

2. Glue the cover stock on the first and last folds.

3. Glue the single sheets to the inside of the remaining folds.

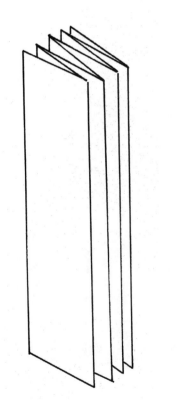
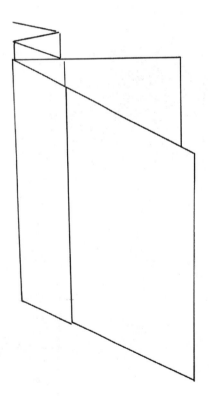

Book with Punch Binding and Fasteners

The construction of this book uses fasteners to hold the pages together. The holes in the pages are made with a paper punch. The instructions are given for an 8-1/2" x 5-1/2" book; any size paper can be used for the lesson.

Supplies

Prong fasteners

10–12 sheets of photocopy paper cut in half

One sheet of cover stock cut in half

One piece of 1" x 8-1/2" cover stock

Paper punch

Instructions

1. Cut the cover stock and photocopy paper into 8-1/2" x 5-1/2" sheets.

2. Punch three holes in the 1" x 8-1/2" cover stock. Use this as a guide and punch all the pages. Once all the pages are punched, stack the photocopy paper. Place a sheet of cover stock on the top and bottom of the stack.

3. Place the 1" x 8-1/2" piece onto the cover. Fasten together with the prong fastener.

4. Additional pages can be added when needed.

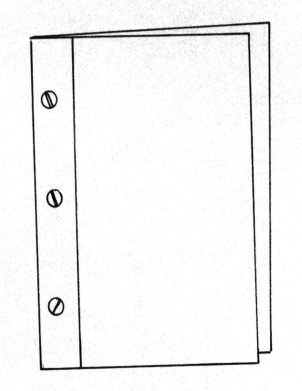

Book with Punch Binding and String

This book uses string or ribbon to hold the pages together. The holes in the pages are made with a paper punch. The instructions are given for an 8-1/2" x 11" book; the instructions can be adapted for any size paper.

Supplies

String

10–20 sheets of photocopy paper

Two sheets of cover stock

One piece of 1" x 11" cover stock in a different color than the larger sheet

Paper punch

Instructions

1. Punch five holes in the 1" x 11" cover stock. Use this as a guide and punch all the pages. Once all the pages are punched, stack the photocopy paper. Place a sheet of cover stock on the top and bottom of the stack.

2. Place the 1" x 11" piece onto the cover. Lace the pages together.

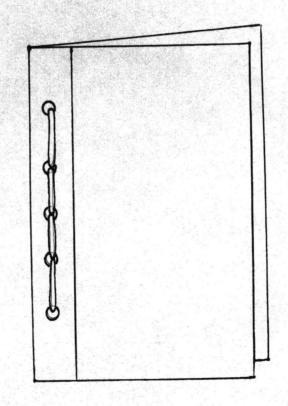

Book with Side-Stitched Binding

This book consists of folded pages stacked inside each other and held together by stitching. The cover is stitched along with the pages.

Supplies

10 sheets of 8-1/2" x 11" photocopy machine paper

Cover stock

Heavy thread

Tapestry needle

Thumbtacks

Instructions

1. Fold each sheet of paper in half, one at a time. Stack all the folded pages inside each other.

2. Fold the cover stock in half and place the stack of folded paper inside.

3. Lay the cover and stacked papers in an open position. With a pencil, lightly mark five holes, evenly spaced. Use a thumbtack to poke through all the layers of paper.

4. Stitch the book together following the illustration.

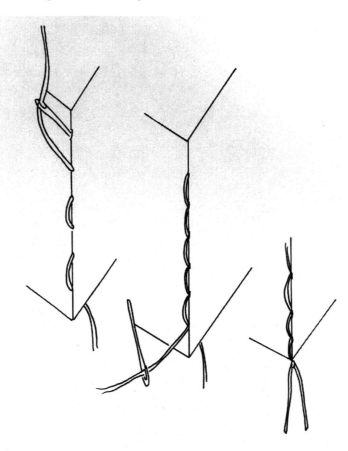

Book with Stub Binding

The pages of a book can be held together using a simple stub binding. The size of the book can be adapted to fit the needs of the project.

Supplies

Five strips of paper 2" x 8-1/2"
Eight sheets of paper 5-1/2" x 8-1/2"
Two sheets of cover stock 5-1/2" x 8-1/2"
Stapler
Glue sticks

Instructions

1. Fold the strips of 2" x 8-1/2" paper in half and stack inside of each other.

2. Staple the strips together on the fold.

3. Glue the 5-1/2" x 8-1/2" paper to the stub.

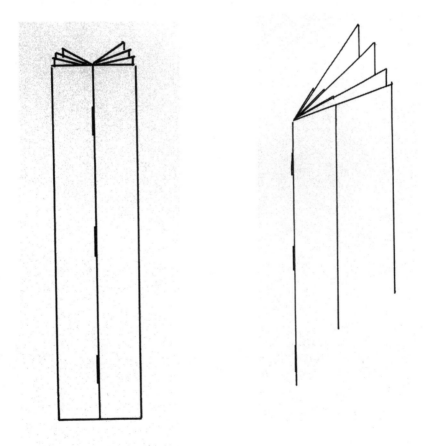

Bubble Paper

Bubbles can be used to make a decorative surface on paper by adding paint to the mixture.

Supplies

Paper

Children's bubbles and wands

Straws

Acrylic paint

Instructions

1. Select the type of paper appropriate for your project. Glossy paper will give a more vibrant effect; mat paper gives a subtle effect.

2. Add color to the bubbles and blow bubbles onto the paper to create the design.

3. A homemade bubble solution can be made by mixing a few drops of paint with four parts of dishwashing detergent and one part water. If wands are not available, a straw can be used to blow air into a bowl of the solution, and the paper can be laid on the surface of the bubbles.

Cinnamon Dough

Decorative clay can be made using cinnamon. Here are two recipes that smell great and require very little preparation. The clay can be air dried and painted. Beads and other decorations can be added to the surface with glue.

Cinnamon Applesauce Dough Recipe

Supplies

One cup applesauce

One cup cinnamon

Mixing bowl

Spoon

Plastic bag

Waxed paper

Rolling pin

Cookie cutters

Instructions

1. Mix the applesauce and the cinnamon together until the mixture resembles cookie dough. Store in a plastic bag if needed.

2. Roll out the dough with a rolling pin to about 1/4" thick.

3. Cut out shapes with cookie cutters; poke a hole in each shape if needed. Set the cut shapes aside on waxed paper for several days, until dry.

4. Paint if desired or add decorations with glue.

Cinnamon Glue Dough Recipe

Supplies

2-1/4 cups ground cinnamon

1/4 cup white glue

1-1/2 cups water

Mixing bowl

Spoon

Plastic bag

Waxed paper

Rolling pin

Cookie cutters

Instructions

1. Set aside 1/4 cup of cinnamon for sprinkling on the work surface. Mix 2 cups of cinnamon in a bowl with the glue, and 3/4 cup of water. Add water as needed, until the mixture resembles cookie dough.

2. Refrigerate for approximately two hours in a plastic bag. Sprinkle some cinnamon on the work surface. Roll out the dough with a rolling pin until about 1/4" thick. Add cinnamon as needed to keep dough from sticking.

3. Cut out shapes with cookie cutters; poke a hole in each shape if needed. Set cut shapes aside on waxed paper for several days, until dry. Paint if desired or add decorations with glue.

Clay for Beads

Beads can be made using this simple recipe. The beads can be decorated by carving designs using a toothpick or other pointed tools. Designs can be also be painted onto the beads using acrylic paint.

Supplies

1/2 cup cornstarch

1/2 cup flour

1/2 cup salt

Warm water

Toothpicks

Acrylic paints

Instructions

1. Mix dry ingredients together. Slowly add warm water until the mixture sticks together and can be shaped.

2. Roll the dough into small balls, make a hole in the balls with a toothpick, and carve decorations into the clay and air dry. Paint if desired and allow shapes to dry.

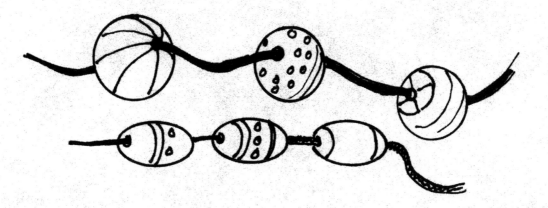

Clay Made with Salt

This recipe makes soft clay that is easy to mold into the desired shapes.

Supplies

1-1/2 cups water

1/2 cup salt

2 teaspoons food coloring

2 tablespoons alum

2 tablespoons cooking oil

2 cups flour

Instructions

Mix water and salt and bring to a boil. Add the food coloring, alum, cooking oil, and flour. Knead together; store in a plastic bag if needed. Air dry after the desired shapes are made.

Collage

Collage is the process of gluing fabric, paper, or found objects to a surface to create a picture. The entire picture can be made using only collage items or the collage can be combined with other material such as drawing, painting, and stamping.

Supplies

Scissors

Glue

Images

Instructions

1. Cut out the images carefully with scissors.

2. Use a glue stick or white glue to attach the images to a surface.

Web Site

The Official Eric Carle Web Site. URL: http://www.eric-carle.com/

Crayon Etching

Traditional scratchboard was originally made using black ink coated on white cardboard. A design was scratched into the dried black ink to expose the white background. Crayon etching uses the same principle. Instead of a white background, the surface is coated with a variety of colors applied with crayons. The colorful background is then coated entirely with black crayon. Sharp tools are used to scratch a design into the black surface.

Supplies

Paper oak tag or poster board

Crayons

Wooden stick, paper clip, or nail for sketching

Instructions

1. Using light-colored crayons, fill the entire paper with color shapes. Once the paper is covered, color over the entire area with black crayon.

2. Scratch a design into the black surface using a sharp tool to expose the colors underneath.

Web Site

Crayola Creativity Center. URL: http://www.crayola.com/

Crayon Rubbing

A textured surface can be transferred to a sheet of paper by placing the paper on the surface and rubbing with a crayon.

Supplies

Paper

Crayons

Textured surfaces

Instructions

1. Place a sheet of paper over a textured surface. Peel the paper from an old crayon.

2. Lay the side of the crayon on the paper and rub to transfer the texture.

Crayon and Sandpaper Print on Fabric

Simple designs drawn with crayons on the surface of sandpaper can be transferred to cloth using a hot iron.

Supplies

Sandpaper

Scissors

Light-colored cotton or muslin fabric

Crayons

Ironing board or a stack of newspapers

Hot iron

Scrap paper

Instructions

1. Cut the sandpaper into the desired size. Pressing heavily, draw the design in crayon on the sandpaper; avoid small details.

2. Prepare the ironing area. Use an ironing board or a stack of newspaper and place the sandpaper design, crayon side down, on the sheet fabric. Place a piece of scrap paper over the back of the sandpaper and heat the image to transfer. Lift the corner to check that the image has transferred completely before lifting off.

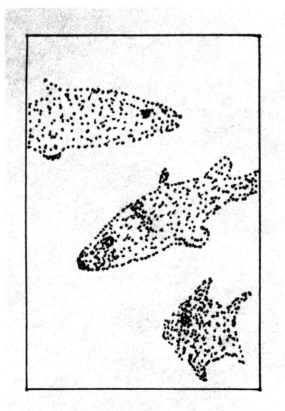

Crayon and Sandpaper Print on Paper

Simple designs drawn with crayons on the surface of sandpaper can be transferred to paper using a hot iron.

Supplies

Sandpaper

Scissors

Paper

Crayons

Ironing board or a stack of newspapers

Hot iron

Scrap paper

Instructions

1. Cut the sandpaper into the desired size. Pressing heavily, draw the design in crayon on the sandpaper; avoid small details.

2. Prepare the ironing area. Use an ironing board or a stack of newspaper and place the sandpaper design, crayon side down, on the sheet of paper. Place a scrap of paper over the back of the sandpaper. Heat the image to transfer. Lift the corner to check that the image has transferred completely before lifting off.

Decorating Sugar Cookies

Supplies

Baked sugar cookies

Icing

Zipper-style sandwich bags

Instructions

1. Fill zipper-style sandwich bags with icing and seal the bag closed.

2. Cut the tip of the bag off to create a small opening. Decorate the cookies by squeezing the icing through the small holes.

Decoupage

Decoupage is the technique of covering the surface of an object using cutout paper shapes. Cardboard boxes and paper shapes can be used as a base.

Supplies

Base shape
White glue
Scissors
Paper images

Instructions

1. Select a variety of images and cut them out without leaving a border. Place glue on the backs of the images and apply them to the shape.

2. Coat the entire surface with the glue.

Dough Made with Glue and Cornstarch

Simple dough that can be made using cornstarch and white glue.

Supplies

1/4 cup white glue

Acrylic paint

1/3 cup cornstarch

Instructions

1. Add a small amount of acrylic paint to the glue before adding the cornstarch.

2. Mix the cornstarch and glue together. Form the small shapes and air dry.

3. Extra dough can be stored in an airtight plastic bag.

Drywall Relief Sculpture

The paper on a sheet of drywall can be removed on one side to provide a surface for carving a design.

Supplies

Small square of drywall approximately 10" x 10"

Spray bottle with water

Pencil

Sticks or large nails for carving

Acrylic paints

Brushes

Instructions

1. Squirt one side of the drywall with water to soak the paper. Peel the paper off on one side only.

2. Draw a simple design on the surface of the plaster. Gently mist the surface of the plaster with water to make carving easier. Use a stick or nail to carve the design. Remember not to carve deeper than half the depth of the plaster.

3. Paint the finished design.

Envelope Template

A variety of papers can be used to make decorative envelopes. Wrapping paper, magazines, newspaper, maps, pages from old books, and construction paper can all be used to make envelopes. An envelope template is provided. The template can be traced onto a cover stock to make it sturdier. Commercially manufactured envelope templates are available. Store-bought envelopes can also be used as a template by carefully peeling apart the glued areas.

Supplies

Photocopy of the envelope template

Assorted paper

Pencil

Scissors

Glue stick

Instructions

1. Place the template on the inside of the selected paper.

2. Trace the template with a pencil. Cut out the shape.

3. Fold and glue to form the envelope.

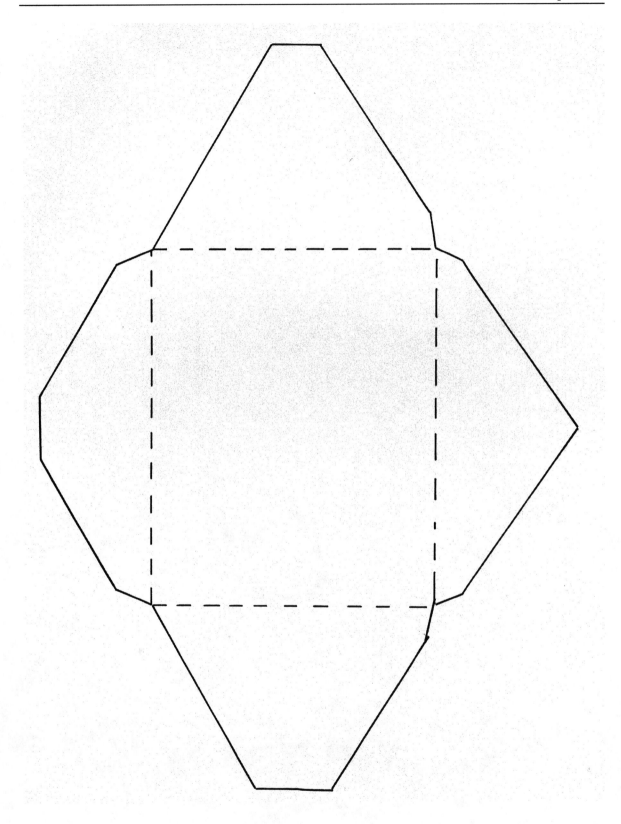

Fabric Appliqué with Stitches

Simple stitches can be used to create pictures using fabric.

Supplies

Fabric
Sewing needles
Thread
Scissors
Pencil
Straight pins

Instructions

1. Draw the desired shapes onto the fabric with pencil. Carefully cut the shapes out of fabric.

2. Pin the shapes to the background fabric.

3. Stitch around the shape.

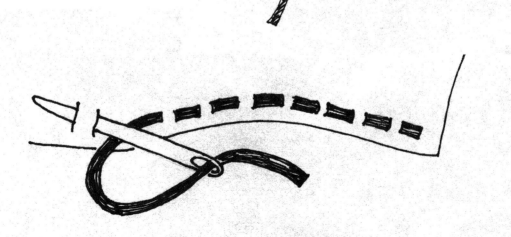

Fabric Appliqué without Stitches

An appliqué design can be created without using any type of sewing. Fusible webbing can be used to attach fabric shapes to a background. Fusible webbing is an adhesive backing that can be attached to fabric with heat. It can be purchased at fabric stores.

Supplies

Fabric

Fusible webbing

Scissors

Pencil

Iron

Ironing surface

Instructions

1. Follow the manufacturer's instructions and attach the fusible webbing to the back of the fabric before it is cut into small shapes. Use a pencil to draw the shape of the object, preferably on the back. Cut out the shape.

2. Use an iron to attach the shape to the background.

Found Object Prints on Fabric

The image of an object can be transferred to fabric. An object can be coated with acrylic paint or ink and pressed carefully to transfer.

Supplies

Found objects
Acrylic paint, ink pads, or paint pads
Paintbrush
Fabric
Newspaper
Scrap paper

Instructions

1. Place the selected object on a sheet of newspaper and coat it with paint or ink.

2. Place the coated object, paint-side down, on the fabric. Press to transfer the paint. Remove the object and repeat.

Found Object Prints on Paper

The image of a found object can be transferred to paper. An object can be coated with acrylic paint or ink and pressed carefully to transfer.

Supplies

Found objects
Tempera or acrylic paint
Paintbrush
Paper
Newspaper
Scrap paper

Instructions

1. Place the found object on a sheet of newspaper and coat it with paint or stamp with ink.

2. Place the coated object, paint-side down, on the paper. Press to transfer the paint. Remove the object and repeat.

Ink Jet Printing on Fabric

Images made on the computer can be transferred onto fabric using a simple technique. The fabric will feed through a printer as long as a stiff backing is applied. Two different types of backing can be used: freezer paper and fusible webbing. The shiny side of freezer paper can be temporarily attached to fabric when heated, making the fabric stiff enough to be fed through a printer. The freezer paper can then be peeled away. Fusible webbing can also be attached to the back of the fabric. When the paper is removed from the fusible webbing, it leaves an adhesive surface on the fabric. The adhesive can be used to mount the printed fabric onto another piece of fabric or paper with heat.

Supplies

Lightweight cotton or muslin

Freezer paper or fusible webbing

Computer image

Ink jet printer

Instructions

1. Have the students make a design on the computer or scan an image into the computer.

2. Cut a piece of fabric and backing approximately 9-1/2" x 12". Iron the shiny side of the freezer paper to the muslin or follow the manufacturer's instructions for adhering the fusible webbing. Trim the adhered paper and fabric to exactly 8-1/2" x 11", and make sure there are no frayed edges.

3. Feed the mounted fabric into the printer and print onto the fabric.

Japanese Suminagashi

Suminagashi is the Japanese word for "ink floating." It is one of the oldest forms of paper marbling. Ink or thinned paints are carefully placed on the surface of a container of water. The color is transferred to the paper by carefully placing the paper on top of the water.

Supplies

Thinned acrylic paint

Tub of water

Paper

Droppers—sticks, toothpicks, eyedroppers, or paintbrushes

Straws

Newspaper

Paper towels

Instructions

1.   Spread newspaper to protect your work area.

2.   Place a layer of paper towels on top of some newspaper in a separate area for drying. Fill a tub halfway with warm water and let it sit so that it is completely still.

3.   Carefully begin dripping small amounts of paint onto the surface of the water. Some colors will spread more than others. Move the colors around by blowing with a straw or swirling with the end of the straw.

4.   Place the paper gently on the surface of the water to transfer the design. Place on the paper towel to dry.

5.   Use a paper towel to skim the surface clean when needed.

Marble and Paint Design

A marble can be rolled through the wet acrylic paint to create a design on a sheet of paper.

Supplies

Shoebox
Paper
Acrylic paint
Marbles

Instructions

1. Cut a sheet of paper to fit in the bottom of a shoebox.

2. Place the sheet of paper in the shoebox along with small drops of paint. Place several marbles in the box and place the lid on the box.

3. Shake the marbles so that they travel through the paint and make a design on the paper.

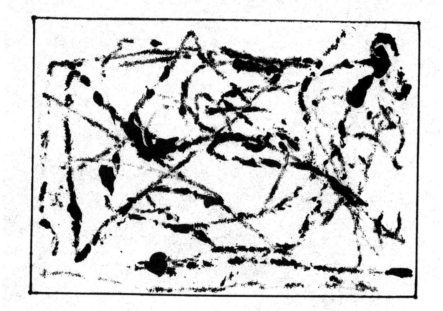

Monoprinting

Monoprinting is a one-of-a-kind image made by applying paint to a smooth surface, such as glass, and transferring the wet image to paper.

Supplies

Acrylic paint

Paintbrushes

Smooth surface

Paper

Instructions

1. Using a paintbrush, apply a design with paint to the smooth surface. Work quickly before the paint dries.

2. Place the paper on the wet paint and rub the back surface of the paper to transfer the paint. Remove the paper and let the image dry.

3. Wipe the area clean and begin again.

Paper Mosaics

Traditional mosaic is the technique of placing small pieces of glass, stone, or ceramic tile in grout. It is one of the oldest forms of creating a picture. Pieces of colored paper can be used to create a similar effect.

Supplies

Pencil

Small strips of colored paper

Black background paper

White glue

Toothpicks

Small scraps of paper for glue

Scissors

Instructions

1. Begin by lightly drawing a design on the background paper with pencil.

2. Place a small amount of glue on the scrap paper.

3. Cut 10–12 small squares from a strip of paper. Place a small amount of glue on the toothpick, dab the toothpick onto the small square of paper, and apply it to the background paper in the desired location.

Paper Punch Collage

There are a large number of paper punches available in a variety of shapes and sizes. The punched shapes can be combined to create a collage.

Supplies

Paper punches

Assorted paper

Glue stick

Instructions

1. Select a variety of punches and paper.

2. Punch the shapes out and carefully glue the pieces to a background paper using a glue stick.

Paper Sculpture

Three-dimensional shapes can be made using torn pieces of paper and wheat paste. Objects such as balloons or plastic bowls can be used as a mold.

Supplies

Strips of newspaper or any lightweight paper

White glue

Water

Container

Base shape

Paints

Brushes

Instructions

1. Cut or tear the paper into strips, no larger than 1-1/2" wide.

2. Mix equal parts of water and white glue in a bowl.

3. Begin dipping the strips of paper in the glue mixture one at a time and placing them onto the base shape. The base can be an inflated balloon, bowl, rolled paper, or rope. Make sure that the strips overlap and cover the entire base shape. Apply three to six layers, depending on how sturdy you want the shape.

4. Allow the paper sculpture to dry overnight. Remove the sculpture from the base shape. Paint the dried surface with acrylic or tempera paints.

Paste Paper

Paste paper is a technique that uses paint mixed with paste to decorate the surface of paper. Textures can be added to the surface by using tools to scrape away areas of paint.

Supplies

Wallpaper paste

Acrylic paint

Mixing container

Wooden spoon or stick

Brushes

Paper

Newspaper

Combs, cardboard scraps, large rubber stamps

Instructions

1. Mix the wallpaper paste using the manufacturer's directions. Be sure to avoid lumps. Add acrylic paint to the mixture.

2. Place a sheet of paper on top of the newspaper. Coat the paper as evenly as possible with the paste mixture.

3. Select a tool and begin creating a design in the wet paste. If you make an error, simply coat the surface with more paste and try again.

Plastic Wrap Backgrounds

Plastic wrap laid on top of wet paint creates an interesting effect on paper.

Supplies

Paper
Brushes
Acrylic paint
Plastic wrap

Instructions

1. Apply a variety of paint colors to the paper using a brush. Cover the entire surface with a heavy coat.

2. Lay a large sheet of plastic wrap over top of the wet surface.

3. Leave the plastic on the surface until the paint dries. Peel the plastic off to uncover the design.

Photocopy Art

Photocopy machines can be used as a creative tool. Multiple copies of one image can be made and manipulated. Copyright-free clip art is available in books and on the Internet. Three-dimensional objects can be placed on the copier to create interesting images.

Supplies

Photocopy machine

Found objects: keys, kitchen gadgets, sewing supplies, art tools, tools, clothing, and photographs

Copyright-free clip art

Drawings

Instructions

Select the images to be photocopied. Place the images on the surface of the photocopy machine and arrange the shapes to the desired layout. Once the images are copied, they can be manipulated with color or other images.

Photocopy on Fabric

Images can be transferred onto fabric using a photocopy machine. The fabric will feed through a photocopy machine as long as a stiff backing is applied. Two different types of backing can be used: freezer paper and fusible webbing. The shiny side of freezer paper can be temporarily attached to fabric when heated, making the fabric stiff enough to be fed through the photocopy machine. The freezer paper can then be peeled away. Fusible webbing can also be attached to the back of the fabric. When the paper is removed from the fusible webbing, it leaves an adhesive surface on the fabric. The adhesive can be used to mount the printed fabric onto another piece of fabric or onto paper with heat.

Supplies

Lightweight cotton or muslin

Fusible webbing or freezer paper

Iron

Black-and-white drawing

Crayons or markers

Instructions

1. Cut a piece of fabric and the backing to approximately 9-1/2" x 12". Attach the backing to the fabric according to the manufacturer's directions.

2. Trim the adhered paper and fabric to exactly 8-1/2" x 11", making sure there are no frayed edges.

3. Place an image in the photocopy machine. Put the stiff fabric into the manual feed of the photocopy machine. Make the photocopy. Add color to the photocopy image using crayons or markers. The fabric can then be adhered to another surface with an iron.

Prints with Fruits and Vegetables on Fabric

Fruits and vegetables can be used to create a variety of images on fabric. Experiment to see if letting the fruits and vegetables dry overnight makes the process easier.

Supplies

Carrots, lemons, mushrooms, peppers, apples, pears

Acrylic paints

Brushes

Paper towels

Fabric

Instructions

Coat one side of the fruit or vegetable with paint and press it onto a sheet of fabric to transfer the image.

Prints with Fruits and Vegetables on Paper

Fruits and vegetables can be used to create a variety of images on paper. Experiment to see if letting the fruits and vegetables dry overnight makes the process easier.

Supplies

Carrots, lemons, mushrooms, peppers, apples, pears

Acrylic paints

Brushes

Paper towels

Paper

Instructions

Coat one side of the fruit or vegetable with paint and press it onto a sheet of paper to transfer the image.

Polymer Clay

Polymer clay comes in many colors, and it can be blended together to create new colors. When heated, the clay becomes hard. It requires low temperatures for firing; this can be done in an oven or toaster oven.

Supplies

Polymer clay

Smooth work surface

Oven

Instructions

1. Begin by kneading to soften the clay.

2. Shape the clay into the desired form. Attach additional shapes and colors by pressing the pieces together.

3. Bake according to the package instructions.

Recycled Foam Tray Prints

Recycled foam trays from the grocery store can be used as a printing surface. Using a dull pencil, a design can be engraved into the surface of the foam tray. Paint coated on the surface will not transfer to a sheet of paper where the image has been engraved.

Supplies

Foam trays

Scissors

Dull pencil

Acrylic paint

Brushes

Paper

Instructions

1. Trim the foam tray so the rim has been removed and the piece is flat.

2. Draw a design into the surface of the tray; press firmly, but do not poke through to the other side.

3. Coat the engraved surface with paint. Place a sheet of paper on top of the painted surface and rub gently to transfer the image.

Rubber Stamping

Stamps are available in a variety of shapes and sizes. Images can be made using pigment inks, dye inks, or paint. Dye-based inks are quick drying and are available in a variety of colors. Pigment inks are slow-drying permanent inks. Pigment ink will not dry on coated paper.

Supplies

Rubber stamps

Ink

Paper

Instructions

1. Select dye or pigment ink. Dab the surface of the stamp image carefully onto the inkpad.

2. Firmly press the coated stamp evenly onto the paper surface.

Scanners

Computer scanners can be used to create artwork. Two-dimensional and three-dimensional objects can be scanned and printed.

Supplies

Scanner with a flat bed

Computer

Printer

Variety of objects

Background paper

Instructions

1.   Select a variety of objects and place them on the bed of the scanner.

2.   Place a background paper on top of the objects.

3.   Scan the objects onto the computer and print the image.

Silk Screening with Freezer Paper

Silk screening is the process of printing multiple images. Ink is forced through an open design in a mesh screen using a squeegee. Freezer paper can be used to learn a simplified form of silk screening. The freezer paper can be adhered to paper or fabric by heating it with an iron. Using a squeegee, paint can be forced through openings in the freezer paper to create a design.

Supplies

Freezer paper

Scissors

Pencil

Acrylic paint

Hot iron

Ironing surface

Cardboard scraps

Instructions

1. Cut an opening in a square of freezer paper leaving a wide border.

2. Iron the freezer paper shiny side down on the fabric.

3. Place a small amount of acrylic paint onto the edge of the freezer paper and using the edge of a piece of scrap cardboard, squeegee the paint over the opening. Remove the freezer paper when the paint is dry.

Soap Carving

Students can explore the basic technique of carving using inexpensive bars of soap. A variety of tools can be used. Plastic knives with a serrated edge work the best. Additional objects such as paper clips, nails, and sticks can also be used.

Supplies

Bar of soap

Sketch paper

Pencil

Carving tools

Newspaper

Instructions

1. Begin by drawing a simple design on the paper.

2. Place newspaper on the work area and begin carving. Remove small amounts of soap at a time.

3. The finished design can be smoothed with a small amount of water rubbed gently over the surface.

Sponge Painting

A sponge can be used as a painting tool. Paint can be applied to a surface with a stamping technique or a brushing technique.

Supplies

Painting surface

Sponges

Acrylic paint

Instructions

1. Decide what type of effect you would like to achieve when using the sponge.

2. Cut the sponge into a small, manageable shape. The sponge can also be cut into a specific shape such as a circle, a triangle, or an animal.

3. Coat the sponge with paint. Dab or brush the paint onto the surface.

Stencils

A stencil is a tool made from a material such as plastic, metal, or cardboard. The material has a cutout shape in the center. Color is transferred through the opening onto a variety of surfaces. A number of the same images can be created using one stencil.

Supplies

Stencil

Paper

Acrylic paint

Sponges

Brushes

Instructions

1. Place the stencil on the surface of the paper or object. Dab the paint into the open area gently with a sponge or brush. Be sure the paint is not too runny; it could drip behind the stencil.

2. Move the stencil to the next spot and repeat. Wipe the stencil clean frequently.

Stuffed Paper Sculpture

Large sheets of paper can be painted and stuffed to create three-dimensional sculptures.

Supplies

Two large sheets of paper

Pencil

Acrylic or tempera paint

Brushes

Water container

Stapler

Scissors

Scrap paper for stuffing

Instructions

1. Ask the students to draw a large shape that fills the entire paper. Paint the entire image. After the paint has dried, cut out the shape and trace it onto the second sheet of paper.

2. Paint the outside surface of the paper and cut out the shape when dry. Staple the two sheets of painted paper together leaving a small opening.

3. Wad small pieces of scrap paper and stuff them into the opening. Staple the opening together.

4. This project can be made using crayons instead of paint.

Watercolor and Salt Design

Salt sprinkled on top of a wet watercolor painting creates an interesting image.

Supplies

Paper

Watercolor paints

Salt

Brushes

Instructions

1. Paint the surface of the paper using a variety of colors. Keep the painting as wet as possible without soaking it.

2. Sprinkle the salt randomly on the painted surface.

3. Remove the salt when the painting has dried.

Part 2

Lessons

Absolutely Normal Chaos

Handmade Journal with a Side-Stitched Binding

Mary Lou is given an assignment for the summer: a journal for her new English teacher. Students can make their own journals for recording the events in their lives.

Supplies

See page 10 for the supply list.

Instructions

1. Follow the instructions on page 10 for making a side-stitched book. Select a method for decorating the cover.

2. Ask the students to begin their journals in the same manner that Mary Lou did: with their names, where they live, and their cast of characters.

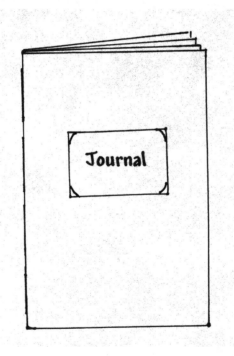

Creech, Sharon. *Absolutely Normal Chaos*. New York: HarperCollins, 1995.

Sharon Creech Website. URL: http://www.sharoncreech.com (Accessed March 26, 2002).

Alice and Greta's Color Magic

Green Photocopy Art

Greta, a naughty witch, casts a spell and causes all the color to drain from the world. Using a black-and-white photocopy, the students can make a picture that has been bewitched.

Supplies

Magazines

Photocopy machine

Green crayon

Instructions

1. Have the students select a picture from a magazine and make a black-and-white photocopy.

2. Students can add color to the picture with green crayon to make the world Greta's favorite color.

Simmons, Steven J. *Alice and Greta's Color Magic*. Illustrated by Cyd Moore. New York: Knopf, 2001.

Steven J. Simmons Website. URL: http://www.aliceandgreta.com/home.html (Accessed March 26, 2002).

The Amazing Days of Abby Hayes: Two Heads Are Better Than One

Quotes

This book is filled with quotes that appear as little notes attached to the pages of the book. The quotes tie into the events in Abby's life. Students can find quotes that relate to their lives and tie the quote into a story along with an illustration.

Supplies

Books with quotes

Lined paper

Drawing paper

Pencil

Instructions

1. Provide the students with an assortment of books with quotes.

2. Ask the students to select a quote and write a true story that relates to the quote.

3. Have the students draw an illustration to go along with the story.

Mazer, Anne. *The Amazing Days of Abby Hayes: Two Heads Are Better Than One.* New York: Scholastic, 2001.

Abbey Hayes Website. URL: http://www.scholastic.ca/titles/abbyhayes/ (Accessed March 26, 2002).

April Wilson's Magpie Magic: A Tale of Colorful Mischief

Drawing with a Magpie

The magpie in the child's drawings comes to life and behaves mischievously. When the child draws a balloon with the orange pencil, the magpie breaks it. The magpie eats the cherry drawn with the red pencil. Students can select a color and draw another object for the magpie.

Supplies

Colored pencils

White drawing paper

Construction paper

Glue

Scissors

Instructions

1. Have the students select a colored pencil and draw an object for the magpie.

2. Ask the students to make a magpie from construction paper to attach to their drawings.

Wilson, April. *April Wilson's Magpie Magic: A Tale of Colorful Mischief*. New York: Dial Books for Young Readers, 1999.

Araminta's Paint Box

Stenciled Art Box

Araminta and her family are moving from their home in Boston to California in a covered wagon. Araminta's uncle gives her a paint box that contains art supplies. She loses the box, but both Araminta and the paint box end up in California. Students can make their own paint box using a sponge, stencils, and acrylic paint.

Supplies

Shoebox

Sponges

Stencils

Acrylic paints

Instructions

1. Have the students coat the outside of their shoeboxes and the lids with paint. Use the sponge to put a thin layer of paint over the entire surface. When the paint is dry, add one or two more coats until the surface is covered.

2. Place the stencil in the desired location and gently sponge the paint to create the design.

Ackerman, Karen. *Araminta's Paint Box.* Illustrated by Betsy Lewin. New York: Atheneum, 1990.

Artemis Fowl

Creating a Secret Code

A code created by the author runs along the bottom of the book's pages. Students can use symbols to create their own codes.

Supplies

White drawing paper

Pencil

Instructions

1. Ask the students to create symbols that stand for words or letters.

2. Have them create a message using the symbols.

Colfer, Eoin. *Artemis Fowl*. New York: Hyperion Books for Children, 2001.

The Eoin Colfer Website. URL: http://www.eoincolfer.com/ (Accessed March 26, 2002).

Arthur Writes a Story

Stretching the Truth

Arthur wants to write a story about how he got his puppy. He stretches the truth to make the story more interesting. Students can write a story about an important event and stretch the truth. Students can include an illustration of their exaggeration.

Supplies

Practice paper
Lined paper
Drawing paper
Pencil

Instructions

1. Ask the students to select an event that is important to them.

2. Write the event on the practice paper as it actually occurred. Have the students go back over their stories and add changes to stretch the truth. Transfer the finished story to the lined paper.

3. Draw a picture to go along with the story.

Brown, Marc. *Arthur Writes a Story*. New York: Little, Brown, 1996.

The Arthur Website. URL: http://pbskids.org/arthur/ (Accessed March 26, 2002).

Arthur's Pet Business

Advertising Signs

Arthur wants to show his parents that he can be responsible. He starts his own pet business and posts signs around the community advertising his business. Students can make their own posters on the computer.

Supplies

Computer

Printer

Paper

Instructions

1. First, have the students decide what type of business they would start.

2. Have the students use the computer to design an advertisement about their business. Print the advertisement when complete.

Brown, Marc. *Arthur's Pet Business.* New York: Little, Brown, 1996.

The Arthur Website. URL: http://pbskids.org/arthur/ (Accessed March 26, 2002).

Ashley Bryan's ABC of African-American Poetry

Alphabet Poetry Book

Ashley Bryan selected lines from poems to make her alphabet book. The class can use the same technique to construct its own alphabet book. The punch-binding technique can be used to bind the book.

Supplies

See the supply list on page 8 for making a punch binding.

White photocopy paper

Practice paper

Pencil

Poetry books

Photocopy machine

Prong fasteners

Paper punch

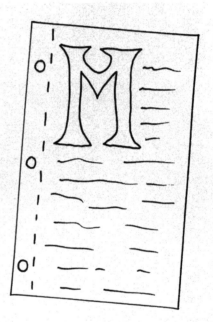

Instructions

1. Provide each student with a sheet of practice paper and a variety of poetry books. Assign each student a letter of the alphabet. Ask them to select a line from a poem that goes with their letter.

2. Ask the students to draw their assigned letter on the photocopy paper with pencil. They can write a line from the poem they selected on the paper along with an illustration. Leave a 1" border on the left side for the binding.

3. Make photocopies of each page, enough copies for each student to construct an entire book. Follow the instructions on page 8 for constructing a punch binding. Select a method to decorate the cover.

Bryan, Ashley. *ABC of African-American Poetry*. New York: Atheneum Books for Young Readers, 1997

1998 Coretta Scott King Illustrators Award Honor Book

The Bad Beginning

Definitions

Throughout the book, the author gives detailed definitions for different words. This gives the reader a very clear understanding of the meaning. Students can find additional words in the story that they can define more clearly.

Supplies

Paper

Pencil

Instructions

1. Ask the students to begin by finding examples in the book of where the author explains different words.

2. Next, have them select words and, using the same writing technique as the author, have them define the words.

Snicket, Lemony. *The Bad Beginning*. Illustrations by Brett Helquist. New York: HarperCollins, 1999.

The Lemony Snicket Website. URL: http://www.lemonysnicket.com/ (Accessed March 26, 2002).

The Bad Beginning

Eye Art Work

Count Olaf's house is filled with artwork of eyes. Count Olaf even has an eye tattooed on his ankle. Students can create their own eye artwork to hang in the Count's house.

Supplies

Paper

Pencil

Crayons

Instructions

Ask the students to create an eye design that could be hung in Count Olaf' s house.

Snicket, Lemony. *The Bad Beginning*. Illustrations by Brett Helquist. New York: HarperCollins, 1999.

The Lemony Snicket Website. URL: http://www.lemonysnicket.com/ (Accessed March 26, 2002).

A Bad Case of Stripes

Colorful Self Portrait

Camilla's body changes colors. She starts out with stripes, first red, white, and blue, and then a variety of color schemes. Students can make self-portraits of how they would look if they were in the same situation as Camilla.

Supplies

Large white drawing paper

Pencil

Crayons

Instructions

1. Provide each student with a large sheet of white paper. Have them draw their self-portraits from the shoulders up.

2. Let the students add colors to their self-portraits with crayon.

Shannon, David. *A Bad Case of Stripes*. New York: Blue Sky Press, 1998.

Birdsong

Report with Decorative Border

Notice the artwork on the pages of the book. The birds are shown in their natural habitats. The borders show the state flowers from the bird's habitat. Students can research a particular bird and write a description about it. Students can draw a border using objects from the bird's habitat such as flowers.

Supplies

White photocopy paper

Lined practice paper

Lined paper

Construction paper

Scissors

Glue

Pencil

Colored pencils

Instructions

1. Have students select a bird, research the selected bird, and write a rough draft. Cut the lined paper approximately 6" x 9". Write the final copy neatly onto the lined paper.

2. Have the students make a bird out of construction paper.

3. Draw the decorative border on the white drawing paper. Add color using the colored pencils.

4. Carefully glue the good copy of the writing in the center of the border. Glue the construction paper bird onto the finished design.

Wood, Audrey. *Birdsong*. Illustrated by Robert Florczak. San Diego: Harcourt Brace, 1997.

Audrey Wood Clubhouse. URL:http://www.audreywood.com/ (Accessed March 26, 2002).

Bring on That Beat

Music Drawing

The illustrations and rhyming text in this book bring to mind the images of jazz music. Students can create images that express their feelings about music they like.

Supplies

Paper

Markers

Instructions

1. Ask the students to select a favorite song.

2. Using a marker, the students can draw shapes that express the sound of the music. Students can add the words from the song to the illustration.

Isadora, Rachael. *Bring on That Beat*. New York: G.P. Putnam's Sons, 2002.

Bud Not Buddy

My Suitcase

Bud carries everything he owns inside his suitcase. Students can draw and list all their prized possessions in their own suitcases.

Supplies

Photocopies of the suitcase pattern

Pencil

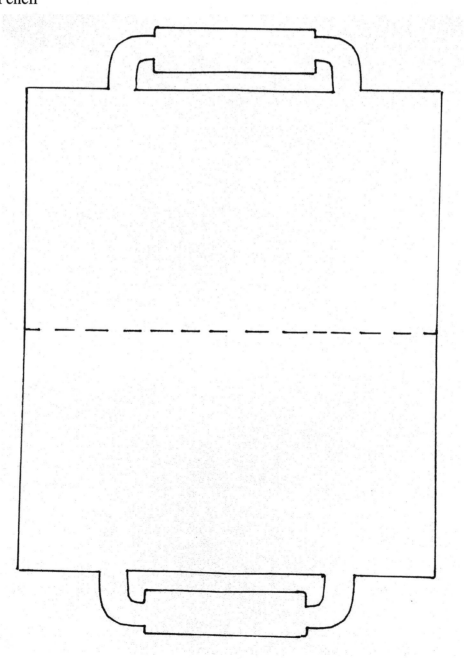

Instructions

1. Provide each student with a photocopy of the suitcase pattern. Have them write a list of all the items in the suitcase that are dear to them.

2. Once the list is completed, have the students draw the items in the suitcase.

Curtis, Christopher Paul. *Bud Not Buddy*. New York: Delacorte Press, 1999.

2000 Newbery Medal Winner

2000 Coretta Scott King Author Award Winner

2001 Coretta Scott King Illustrators Award Winner

The Bunyans

Collage

The illustrations show the Bunyan family's size compared to ordinary objects. Students can use collage to make a picture that shows the size of the Bunyan family.

Supplies

Magazines

Background paper

Scissors

Glue

Instructions

1. Provide the students with an assortment of magazines. Ask them to find pictures that they can combine to make a collage showing how big the Bunyans are compared to normal objects.

2. Cut the pictures out and glue them onto a background paper.

Wood, Audrey. *The Bunyans*. Illustrated by David Shannon. New York: Blue Sky Press/Scholastic, 1996.

Audrey Wood Clubhouse. URL: http://www.audreywood.com/ (Accessed March 26, 2002).

Can You See What I See?
Picture Puzzles to Search and Solve

Assemblage Bulletin Board with Clues

This book asks "Can you see what I see?" and gives clues in rhyme. Students can create their own group assemblage for a bulletin board along with clues. Assemblage is the art of placing three-dimensional objects in an arrangement.

Supplies

Found objects from home

Background papers: wrapping paper, magazine pictures, labels from canned food, cereal boxes, and advertisements.

Staples

Glue

Pins

Thumbtacks

Note cards

Bulletin board

Instructions

1. Suggest items such as small plastic toys from fast-food restaurants, toys from bubble gum–type machines, small pieces from old board games, old kitchen gadgets, sewing items, play jewelry, and old art supplies.

2. Place a variety of papers on the bulletin board as a background.

3. Ask the students to begin attaching their objects to the bulletin board. The light objects can be glued in place; the heavier objects will need to be secured with tacks, staples, or pins.

4. Have the students write their clues on the note cards.

Wick, Walter. *Can You See What I See? Picture Puzzles to Search and Solve.* New York: Scholastic, 2002.

Can You Top That?

Exaggerated Animal Drawing

The children in this story compete to see who can draw the most impressive animal. Students can have their own competition and exaggerate an animal.

Supplies

White drawing paper

Pencil

Crayons

Instructions

1. Ask the students to select an animal they would like to draw and have them exaggerate the animal's features.

2. Have the students give the animal a new name that goes with its new appearance.

Nikola, Lisa, W. *Can You Top That?* Illustrated by Hector Viveros Lee. New York: Lee & Low Books, 2000.

Lisa W. Nikola Website. URL: http://www.nikolabooks.com/ (Accessed March 26, 2002).

Charlotte's Web

Glitter Spider Web with Adjectives

Charlotte made her spider web with words that described Wilbur. Students can create their own spider web using glue and glitter. Adjectives describing the student's personality can be written on the web.

Supplies

Pencil
Black construction paper
Glue
Glitter

Instructions

1. Have the students decide which adjectives they want to include on their spider web. Draw a web on the black paper with pencil. Include one or two adjectives in the design. Caution the students about writing the letters too small and close; it will make gluing difficult.

2. Apply glue over the top of the pencil lines and sprinkle the wet glue with glitter.

White, E.B. *Charlotte's Web*. Illustrated by Garth Williams. New York: Harper & Row, 1952.

Cinderella Skeleton

Halloween Tale and Drawing

This story is a Halloween version of the classic tale of Cinderella. Students can select a classic tale to write and illustrate with a Halloween theme.

Supplies

Lined practice paper

Lined paper

White drawing paper

Pencil

Instructions

1. Ask the students to select a tale they would like to write with a Halloween theme. Have them begin with a rough draft on the lined practice paper.

2. Once the students have a version they are happy with, they can transfer the finished writing to the lined paper.

3. Students can use pencil to illustrate a character from their tale.

San Souci, Robert D. *Cinderella Skeleton*. Illustrated by David Catrow. San Diego: Silver Whistle/ Harcourt, 2000.

Robert San Souci Website. URL: http://www.rsansouci.com/ (Accessed March 26, 2002).

Cindy Ellen: A Western Cinderella

Western Tale and Drawing

This is the Western variation of the classic Cinderella. Students can select a classic tale to write and illustrate with a Western theme.

Supplies

Lined practice paper

Lined paper

White drawing paper

Pencil

Instructions

1. Ask the students to select a tale they would like to write with a Western theme. Have them begin with a rough draft on the lined practice paper.

2. Once they have a version they are happy with, they can transfer the finished writing to the lined paper.

3. Students can use pencil to make an illustration of a character from their tale.

Lowell, Susan. *Cindy Ellen: A Wild Western Cinderella*. Illustrated by Jane Manning. New York: HarperCollins, 2000.

Click, Clack, Moo: Cows That Type

Students' List of Demands on Cow Stationery

Farmer Brown's cows find a typewriter and begin making demands. When the farmer doesn't give them what they want, they go on strike. Students can type a list of their own demands for how they would like their school rules to change. Students can make cow stationery for their list.

Supplies

Computer with a word processing program

White printer paper

Printer

Pencil

Black marker

Instructions

1. Have the students type a list of wishes or demands they would like to share with their principal.

2. Using black marker, have the students decorate the borders of the white photocopy paper with cow images. Print the list onto the cow stationery using a printer.

Cronin, Doreen, *Click, Clack, Moo: Cows That Type*. Illustrated by Betsy Lewin. New York: Simon & Schuster Books for Young Readers, 2000.

Cook-a-Doodle-Doo!

Favorite Recipe and Drawing

Big Brown Rooster gets help from all his friends when he tries to make strawberry short-cake. But his friends do not know how to cook. Students can rewrite their favorite recipes with detailed instructions and draw a picture of how the food looks.

Supplies

Recipe from home

Lined practice paper

Pencil

Lined paper

White drawing paper

Instructions

1. Have the students bring in a favorite recipe from home. On the practice paper, have them rewrite the recipe using detailed step-by-step instructions to help their friends cook.

2. Write the final copy on the lined paper along with an illustration.

Stevens, Janet and Susan Stevens Crummel. *Cook-a-Doodle-Doo!* Illustrated by Janet Stevens. San Diego: Harcourt Brace, 1999.

Janet Stevens Website. URL: http://www.janetstevens.com/ (Accessed March 26, 2002).

Crocodile! Crocodile! Stories Told Around the World

Folktales Retold with Cut Paper Borders

The author has taken six folktales from other cultures and retold them in her own words. The illustrator uses cut paper for the artwork. Students can select their favorite folktale to retell in their own words and create a cut-paper border similar to the type that the artist used. The design can be achieved using paper punches, a variety of colors, and repeating shapes.

Supplies

Folktale books

Lined practice paper

Lined paper

Pencil

Strips of colored paper

Scraps of construction paper

Paper punches

Glue

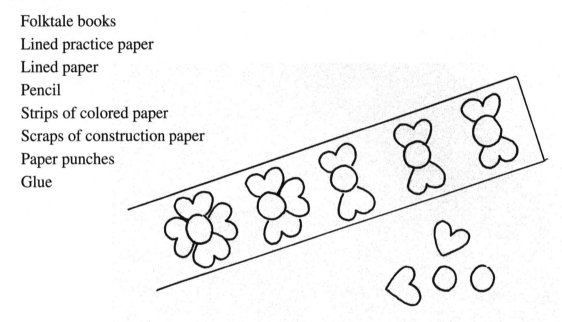

Instructions

1. Have the students use the practice paper to write the rough draft of their version of a folktale; they can transfer the final copy to the lined paper. Ask them to leave a space around the outside of the paper to place the border.

2. Examine the borders the artist used to decorate the pages of the book. Provide the students with four strips of colored paper that fit around the outside edge of the white lined paper. Attach the strips around the outer edge of the paper with glue.

3. Give the students small scraps of construction paper for punching out shapes. Punch out shapes from the small pieces of paper and glue them onto the border in a design.

Baumgartner, Barbara. *Crocodile! Crocodile! Stories Told Around the World.* Illustrated by Judith Moffatt. London; New York: D Kindersley, 1994.

Barbara Baumgartner Website. URL: http://www.barbarastories.com/ (Accessed March 26, 2002).

Cuddly Dudley

Polymer Clay Penguin

Dudley the penguin wants to be left alone, but he is so cuddly that no one can stop cuddling him. Students can make a small Dudley from black and white polymer clay.

Supplies

White and black polymer clay

Instructions

1. Have the students begin by kneading the clay.
2. Roll the white clay into an egg shape.
3. Flatten the black pieces of clay and shape into wings.
4. Attach the wings and make additional details.
5. Bake according to manufacturer's instructions.

Alborough, Jez. *Cuddly Dudley*. Cambridge, MA: Candlewick Press, 1995.

Sea World Website. URL: http://www.seaworld.org (Accessed March 26, 2002).

Dear First Grade Journal

Stub Binding Journal

This book contains entries in Junie B's first-grade journal. Students can make their own journals and write their own entries.

Supplies

See page 11 for supplies.

Instructions

1. Follow the instructions on page 11 for making a stub-binding journal. Select a method to decorate the cover.

2. Have the students write in their journals daily.

Park, Barbara. *Dear First Grade Journal.* Illustrated by Denise Brunkus. New York: Random House, 2001.

Kids at Random. URL: http://www.randomhouse.com/kids/junieb/books.html (Accessed March 26, 2002).

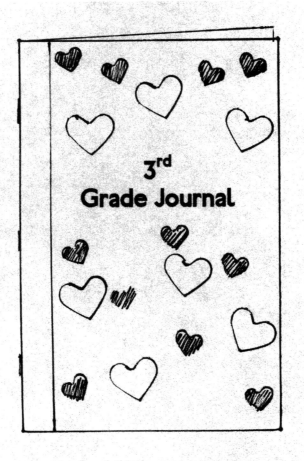

Dear Peter Rabbit

Letter to Book Characters Using Artistamps

Artistamps are fake postage stamps created by artists. They are used next to legal postage stamps and have the appearance of real stamps. The story presents letters written by fairy-tale characters to each other. Students can write letters to book characters and use the fake postage stamps on the envelopes.

Supplies

Photocopy of the stamp pattern on page 2

Pencil

Colored pencils

Thumbtacks

Lined paper

Envelopes

Instructions

1. Make a copy of the stamp pattern. Follow the instructions on page 2 for making artistamps.

2. Ask the students to write their letters to a fairy-tale character, being sure to include all the elements of a personal letter.

3. Have the students place the finished letter into an envelope that is properly addressed. Place the artistamp on the envelope.

Ada, Alma Flor. *Dear Peter Rabbit*. Illustrated by Leslie Tryon. New York: Atheneum, 1994.

Alma Flor Ada Website. URL: http://www.almaada.com/ (Accessed March 26, 2002).

The Diary of Melanie Martin

Handmade Diary

Melanie writes about her family vacation to Italy. Students can make a diary to write about their own experiences.

Supplies

See page 10 for the supply list.

Instructions

1. Follow the instructions on page 10 for constructing a side-stitched book.

2. Select a method to decorate the cover.

3. Once the book is completed, have the students begin writing daily in their diaries.

Weston, Carol. *The Diary of Melanie Martin*. New York: Knopf, 2000.

Carol Weston Website. URL: http://www.carolweston.com/ (Accessed March 26, 2002).

Does a Kangaroo Have a Mother, Too?

Paste Paper Animals

Students can make animals similar to the ones in Eric Carle's book using the paste paper technique. Paste paper uses paint mixed with paste to decorate the surface of paper. Textures can be added to the surface by using tools to scrape away areas of paint. Students can research animals and write a description.

Supplies

See page 39 for the supply list.

Pencil

Scissors

Lined paper

Instructions

1. Follow the instructions on page 39 for paste paper.

2. Once the paste paper is dry, have the students draw and cut out an animal shape.

3. Have the students write their description on the lined paper.

Carle, Eric. *Does a Kangaroo Have a Mother, Too?* New York: HarperCollins, 2000.

The Official Eric Carle Website. URL: http://www.eric-carle.com/ (Accessed March 26, 2002).

Doodle Dandies:
Poems That Take Shape

Shape Poems

This book contains a collection of poems that appear in the shape of the subject. Students can write poems using the same technique.

Supplies

Pencil

Practice paper

White drawing paper

Instructions

1. Have the students select a topic.

2. Make several illustrations to go along with the poem.

3. Use the white drawing paper for the finished work.

Lewis, J. Patrick. *Doodle Dandies: Poems That Take Shape*. Illustrated by Lisa Desimini. New York: Atheneum Books for Young Readers, 1998.

Patrick Lewis Home Page. URL: http://www.jpatricklewis.com/ (Accessed March 26, 2002).

Dr. Pompo's Nose

Pumpkin Faces

The characters in the book are created using pumpkins. Students can create their own characters using pumpkins.

Supplies

Small pumpkins

Black markers

Instructions

1. Provide each student with a small pumpkin.

2. Have them use the stem as the pumpkin's nose and draw eyes and a mouth on the pumpkin using the black marker.

Freymann, Saxton and Joost Elffers. *Dr. Pompo's Nose*. New York: Scholastic, 2000.

The Dream Shop

Dream Collage

Joseph and Pip visit a shop where they can purchase dreams. Students can create a collage inside a box that contains the items they would shop for in their dreams.

Supplies

Magazine

Scissors

Glue

Cardboard box

Instructions

1.   Ask the students to find pictures and words in magazines that describe the things they would purchase if they could shop in their dreams.

2.   Glue the cut shapes inside the box.

Kenah, Katharine. *The Dream Shop.* Illustrated by Peter Catalanotto. New York: HarperCollins, 2002.

Duke Ellington:
The Piano Prince and His Orchestra

Crayon Etching

The illustrations in this book strongly express the sound of the instruments using a scratchboard or crayon etching technique. Students can use this technique to create their own images of sound.

Supplies

Paper oak tag or poster board

Crayons

Wooden stick, paper clip, or nail for sketching

Instructions

1. Follow the instructions on page 18 for making a crayon etching.

2. Scratch a design into the black using a tool to expose the colors underneath to express music.

Pinkney, Andrea Davis. *Duke Ellington: The Piano Prince and His Orchestra*. Illustrated by Brian Pinkney. New York: Hyperion Books for Young Children, 1998.

1999 Coretta Scott King Illustrators Award Honor Book

Eek! Creek! Snicker, Sneak

Creatures

The artist created the two creatures from his imagination. Bugbear and Bugaboo are images he invented. Students can create a pair of creatures that make noise in the night and then name them.

Supplies

Paper

Pencil

Markers

Instructions

1. Ask the students to create two creatures.

2. Invent names for the creatures and describe the sounds they make in the night.

Green, Rhonda Gowler. *Eek! Creek! Snicker, Sneak.* Illustrated by Jos. A. Smith. New York: Atheneum Books for Young Readers, 2002.

Emily Dickinson's Letter to the World

Book with a Stub Binding and Poems by Emily Dickinson

This book has a brief description about the life of Emily Dickinson and includes a selection of her poems. Students can make a book with a stub binding and their favorite poems by Emily Dickinson.

Supplies

See page 11 for the supply list

Emily Dickinson poetry books

Pencil

Instructions

1. Follow the instructions on page 11 for constructing a book with a stub binding. Select a method to decorate the cover.

2. Ask the students to select their favorite Emily Dickinson poem and write the poems on the book's pages.

Winter, Jeanette. *Emily Dickinson's Letter to the World.* New York: Frances Foster Books, 2002.

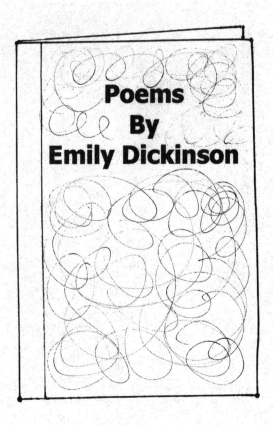

Ernest L. Thayer's Casey at Bat

Scrapbook Page

The book gives the appearance of a very old scrapbook. The artist includes a variety of memorabilia. Students can create a scrapbook page that contains memorabilia from a local event.

Supplies

Memorabilia from home

Glue

Cover stock paper

Pencil

Instructions

1. Ask the students to bring in objects to construct a scrapbook page. Suggest photographs, newspaper clippings, ticket stubs, programs, or any flat keepsake.

2. Provide each student with a sheet of heavy cover stock. Ask the students to arrange the pieces on the cover stock.

3. Once they have an arrangement they like, have the students glue the pieces in place and write captions.

Bing, Christopher H. *Ernest L. Thayer's Casey at Bat*. New York: Handprint Books, 2000.

Everything to Spend the Night
—from A to Z

List to Spend the Night

Students can compose a list of objects from A to Z that they would take to spend the night at someone's house.

Supplies

Suitcase pattern on page 70

Pencil

Instructions

1. Provide each student with a photocopy of the suitcase pattern.

2. Ask the students to write and draw all the items they would take for a sleepover, making sure they use all the letters of the alphabet.

Paul, Ann Whitford. *Everything to Spend the Night—from A to Z*. Illustrated by Maggie Smith. New York: DK Publishers, 1999.

Fiona's Private Pages

Handmade Journal

Fiona describes her friendships in a journal. Students can make a side-stitched journal to write about their own friendships.

Supplies

See page 10 for the supply list.

Instructions

1. Follow the instructions on page 10 for constructing a side-stitched book.

2. Select a method to decorate the cover.

3. Once the book is completed, have the students begin writing daily in their journals.

Cruise, Robin. *Fiona's Private Pages*. San Diego: Harcourt, 2000.

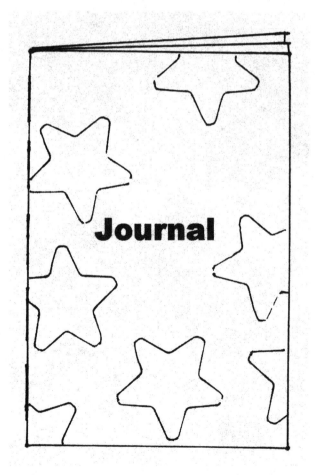

Flat Stanley

Decorative Envelopes

Flat Stanley is a story about a young boy who is flattened when a bulletin board falls on top of him. He travels in an envelope. Using the envelope pattern and a variety of papers, students can create their own envelopes for Flat Stanley's travels. Have the students draw a Flat Stanley paper doll to travel inside the envelope. Instruct students on the proper method of addressing an envelope.

Supplies

Wrapping paper, newspaper, magazines, or other papers

Photocopy of envelope pattern

Scissors

Pencil

Glue stick

Construction paper for Flat Stanley

Instructions

1. Have the students select the type of paper they would like to use for their envelope. Trace the envelope pattern onto the back of the paper.

2. Cut out the envelope. Glue carefully with a glue stick.

3. Give the students assorted pieces of construction paper to make a Flat Stanley figure.

4. Have the students address the envelope.

Brown, Jeff. *Flat Stanley*. Illustrated by Steve Bjorkman. New York: HarperTrophy, 1996.

The Flat Stanley Project. URL: http://flatstanley.enoreo.on.ca/index.htm (Accessed March 26, 2002).

Flat Stanley

Artistamp Design

Artistamps are fake postage stamps created by artists. They are used next to legal postage stamps and have the appearance of real stamps. Students can create their own artistamps for Flat Stanley's envelope.

Supplies

See page 2 for the list of supplies

Instructions

1. Follow the instructions on page 2 for making artistamps.

2. Place the artistamp on Flat Stanley's envelope.

Brown, Jeff. *Flat Stanley*. Illustrated by Steve Bjorkman. New York: HarperTrophy, 1996.

The Flat Stanley Project. URL: http://flatstanley.enoreo.on.ca/index.htm (Accessed March 26, 2002).

From the Mixed-up Files of Mrs. Basil E. Frankweiler

Plans for Hiding

Claudia decides to run away and plans it very carefully. Students can research a different location for Claudia to hide out.

Supplies

Brochures

Lined paper

Pencil

Instructions

1. Provide the students with brochures from museums, zoos, aquariums, or science centers.

2. Ask the students to write a plan showing how Claudia could hide for a few days.

Konigsburg, E.L. *From the Mixed-up Files of Mrs. Basil E. Frankweiler.* New York: Atheneum Books for Young Readers, 1967.

The Gardener

Stenciled Planter

Lydia's father is out of work and she must move to the city with her Uncle Jim. Lydia has a love for planting flowers. Students can decorate planters to grow flowers in the classroom.

Supplies

Garden planters
Acrylic paints
Stencils
Sponges
Potting soil
Seeds

Instructions

1.   Divide the students into groups. Follow the instructions on page 52 for using a stencil. Demonstrate how to place the stencil on the surface and apply the paint using a sponge.

2.   After the entire surface is decorated, plant an assortment of flowers in the decorated planters.

Stewart, Sarah. *The Gardener.* Illustrated by David Small. New York: Farrar, Straus & Giroux, 1997.

Ghost Canoe

Bone Game Pieces

The bone game is played by the Makah and Nitinat men; they hide bone pieces in each hand. The shapes are identical except one has a black band. The object of the game is to guess which hand holds the unmarked piece. Students can make their own game pieces from polymer clay.

Supplies

Polymer clay

Black string

Instructions

1. Ask the students to soften the clay by kneading.

2. Have the students make two identical shaped pieces, they should fit into a closed hand.

3. Bake the clay according to the manufactures instructions. Add the black string to one of the pieces.

Hobbs, Will. *Ghost Canoe.* New York: Avon Books, 1997.

Will Hobbs Official Website. URL: http://www.willhobbsauthor.com/ (Accessed March 26, 2002).

Giggle Bugs

Interactive Greeting Card

Giggle Bugs is an interactive book that entertains and surprises the reader. Students can make an interactive greeting card using flaps.

Supplies

Card stock 8-1/2" x 11"

2" x 2" square of cardstock

Pencils

Glue sticks

Markers

Instructions

1. Have the students begin by folding the 8-1/2" x 11" cardstock in half. Fold the edge of the 2" x 2" square of cardstock.

2. Glue the flap to the inside of the card.

3. Next, have the students draw a design on the front of the card along with a message.

4. Then draw a design on the inside of the card along with a surprise under the flap.

Carter, David A. *Giggle Bugs*. New York: Little Simon, 1999.

Popup Books By Carter Website. URL: http://www.popupbooks.com/ (Accessed March 26, 2002).

Gingerbread Baby

Cinnamon Dough Gingerbread Baby

This story is similar to the tale of the gingerbread man, except this story is about a gingerbread baby. Students can make their own gingerbread baby with self-hardening dough.

Supplies

Cinnamon dough recipe on page 13

Paints in small squeeze bottles

Gingerbread man cookie cutter

Instructions

1. Prepare the cinnamon dough according to the recipe. Roll the dough into a flat sheet and use the cookie cutter to make a gingerbread man shape.

2. Let the shape dry overnight.

3. Use paints in the squeeze bottle to decorate the figures.

Brett, Jan. *Gingerbread Baby*. New York: Putnam, 1999.

The Jan Brett Home Page. URL: http://www.janbrett.com/ (Accessed March 26, 2002).

Grandfather Tang's Story

Animal Design with Tangrams

Tangrams are ancient Chinese puzzles. The tangrams in the story are arranged into the shapes of animals. Students can make their own tangrams and make a variety of animal shapes.

Supplies

Photocopy of the tangram pattern

Scissors

Instructions

1. Provide each student with a photocopy of the tangram pattern.

2. Ask the students to cut the shapes apart and experiment to create animal shapes.

Tompert, Ann. *Grandfather Tang's Story*. Illustrated by Robert Andrew Parker. New York: Crown Publishers, 1990.

The Graphic Alphabet

Creative Alphabet

The artist, David Pelletier, uses the natural shape of the letters of the alphabet to express the meaning of words beginning with that letter. Students can use this method to create letters of the alphabet like the artist.

Supplies

Practice paper

Drawing paper

Pencil

Instructions

1. Assign each student a letter of the alphabet. Instruct the students to select several words they would like to illustrate.

2. Let the students experiment with the words on practice paper. Once the students have found a design they like, have them make a final design on the drawing paper.

3. The pages can be displayed individually or photocopies can be made and bound into books using the punch binding method on pages 8 or 9.

Pelletier, David. *The Graphic Alphabet*. New York: Orchard, 1996.

Gus and Button

Food Characters

All of the pictures in the book were made using food. They were photographed and then collaged. Students can make their own characters using images of food.

Supplies

Magazines

Scissors

Glue

Paper

Instructions

1. Ask the students to find images of food and body elements in magazines. Combine the food images with the body parts to create characters.

2. Glue the shapes to the paper.

Freymann, Saxton and Joost Elffers. *Gus and Button*. New York: Scholastic, 2001.

Ha! Ha! Ha!
1,000 Jokes, Riddles, Facts and More

Knock-Knock Joke

Students can illustrate their own knock-knock jokes using a door made from construction paper.

Supplies

Construction paper
Pencil
Paper

Instructions

1. Ask the students to first select a joke. Construct a door using the construction paper.

2. Glue the door to the background paper so that the door opens. Write the knock-knock joke on the outside of the door and the answer on the inside.

Thomas, Lyn. *Ha! Ha! Ha! 1,000 Jokes, Riddles, Facts and More.* Illustrated by Dianne Eastman. Toronto: Owl Books, 2001.

Harold and the Purple Crayon

Drawing with Purple Crayon

Harold uses his purple crayon to take a walk. Students can take a walk on paper using a purple crayon in an accordion book.

Supplies

Supplies from page 6

Purple crayons

Instructions

1. Follow the instructions on page 6 for constructing an accordion book.

2. Have the students use the purple crayon to take a walk in their books.

Johnson, Crockett. *Harold and the Purple Crayon*. New York: HarperCollins, 1955.

The Crockett Johnson Home Page. URL: http://www.ksu.edu/english/nelp/purple/ (Accessed March 26, 2002).

Harry Potter and the Goblet of Fire

Acronyms Badges

Hermione makes badges with the acronym S.P.E.W., which stands for the Society for the Promotion of Elfish Welfare. Students can make their own badges using an acronym.

Supplies

Pencil

Paper

Colored pencil

Circle pattern

Cardboard

Glue stick

Pin backs

Instructions

1. Ask the students to invent an acronym.

2. Have the students draw a circle shape on the drawing paper. Next, draw the letters on the drawing paper. Add color to the design with colored pencils.

3. Cut the circle out and glue it to a cardboard circle. Add a pin back to the back of the cardboard circle.

Rowling, J.K. *Harry Potter and the Goblet of Fire*. New York: Scholastic, 2000.

The Official Harry Potter Website. URL: http://harrypotter.warnerbros.com/home.html (Accessed March 26, 2002).

Scholastic's Harry Potter Home Page. URL: http://www.scholastic.com/harrypotter/home.asp (Accessed March 26, 2002).

Henny Penny

Collage

On their way to warn the King that the sky is falling, Henny Penny and her friends pass by famous landmarks. Students can use a collage to make their own picture.

Supplies

Magazines

Scissors

Glue

Paper

Instructions

1. Provide students with an assortment of magazines. It may be necessary to give the students a photocopy of a chicken or other birds, as it may be difficult for all the students to find a picture in the magazines.

2. Have the students cut out the pictures and glue them onto the background paper.

Wattenberg, Jane. *Henny Penny*. New York: Scholastic, 2000.

Hey You! C'mere: A Poetry Slam

Description and Illustration

The poem "Great Granma" uses words that give the reader a picture that describes Great Granma. Students can select a person to describe and use the same format the author did. Students can also include an illustration.

Supplies

Paper

Pencil

Instructions

1. Ask the students to begin by selecting a person they would like to write about.

2. Have the students write their poems and include an illustration.

Swados, Elizabeth. *Hey You! C'mere: A Poetry Slam.* Illustrated by Joe Cepeda. New York: Scholastic, 2002.

Hey You! C'mere: A Poetry Slam

Onomatopoeia Poem

Words that describe real sounds are called onomatopoeia. The poem "Storm" uses onomatopoeia. Students can write and illustrate their own poems using onomatopoeia.

Supplies

Paper

Pencil

Instructions

1. Ask the students to select a topic for their poems.

2. Have the students write their poems using as much onomatopoeia as possible. Ask the
    students to include an illustration with their poems.

Swados, Elizabeth. *Hey You! C'mere: A Poetry Slam.* Illustrated by Joe Cepeda. New York:
Scholastic, 2002.

The Hopeful Trout and Other Limericks

Illustrated Limerick

Limericks are humorous five-line poems. Students can write and illustrate their own limericks.

Supplies

Practice paper

Drawing paper

Pencil

Instructions

1. Students can begin their limericks on practice paper. The rhyme scheme is a-a-b-b-a. Suggest that the students begin with: *There once was a*, *There was an*, or *I once knew a*.

2. The students can transfer their best limericks to the white paper and draw an illustration.

Ciardi, John. *The Hopeful Trout and Other Limericks*. Illustrated by Susan Meddaugh. Boston: Houghton Mifflin, 1989.

The Online Poetry Classroom. URL: http://www.onlinepoetryclassroom.org/ (Accessed March 26, 2002).

The Academy of American Poets Website. URL: http://www.poets.org/poets/index.cfm (Accessed March 26, 2002).

The Hundred Penny Box

Decoupage Box

Great-great-Aunt Dew used a wooden box to hold one penny for every year of her life. Students can create keepsake boxes to hold their own pennies.

Supplies

Small box

Assortment of paper pieces

Scissors

White glue

Brush

Instructions

1. Ask the students to bring in a variety of paper from home: newspaper clippings, magazine pictures, copies of photographs, ticket stubs, and greeting cards.

2. Have the students cut the papers to the size and shapes they like. Apply glue to the surface of the box, and place the cut paper onto the glue. Coat the surface of the paper with glue. Continue to add additional shapes next to and overlapping each other to cover the entire box.

Mathis, Sharon Bell. *The Hundred Penny Box*. Illustrated by Leo and Diane Dillon. New York: Puffin Books, 1986.

I Spy Spooky Night:
A Book of Picture Riddles

I Spy Group Collage

The author uses rhyming clues to give the reader information to search for specific objects. The objects are cleverly hidden in the picture. Students can make an I Spy bulletin board design using collage.

Supplies

Bulletin board covered with paper

Magazines

Scissors

Glue

Note cards

Instructions

1.   Ask the class to select a theme for the bulletin board. Use a topic that would naturally have a lot of objects, such as a junkyard, a haunted house, or a child's playroom.

2.   Ask each student to select images they would like to hide in the group collage. The key is to have all of the images they select rhyme. Cut a variety of additional pictures from magazines. Cut carefully around the object omitting the background.

3.   Glue all the items from the entire class onto the bulletin board paper. Have the students write their clues in rhymes on note cards.

Marzollo, Jean. *I Spy Spooky Night: A Book of Picture Riddles*. Photographs by Walter Wick. New York: Scholastic, 1996.

Jean Marzollo Website. URL: http://www.jeanmarzollo.com/ (Accessed March 26, 2002).

I Spy Year Round Challenger!

I Spy Assemblage Bulletin Board

Assemblage is the art of placing three-dimensional objects in an arrangement. Students can make an I Spy bulletin board design using the assemblage technique. The students can include rhyming clues to give the reader information to search for specific objects.

Supplies

Found objects from home

Bulletin board covered with paper

Staples

Glue

Pins

Thumbtacks

Note cards

Paper for envelopes

Instructions

1. Ask the students to bring a variety of small objects from home to use on the bulletin board. Suggest items such as small plastic toys from fast-food restaurants, toys from bubble gum–type machines, small pieces from old board games, old kitchen gadgets, sewing items, play jewelry, and old art supplies.

2. Place a variety of papers on the bulletin board as a background.

3. Ask the students to begin attaching their objects to the bulletin board. The light objects can be glued in place; the heavier objects will need to be secured with tacks, staples, or pins.

4. Have the students write their clues on the note cards.

Marzollo, Jean. *I Spy Year Round Challenger!* Photographs by Walter Wick. New York: Scholastic, 1996.

Jean Marzollo Website. URL: http://www.jeanmarzollo.com/ (Accessed March 26, 2002).

Insectlopedia

Brown Paper Insects

Doug Florian used brown paper bags and watercolors to paint the images of his insects. The book contains 20 short poems about insects. Students can construct large bugs from brown paper bags and watercolor paints. They can write a descriptive poem about an insect on their paintings.

Supplies

Brown paper bags

Watercolor paints

Brushes

Pencil

Practice writing paper

Instructions

1.   Ask the students to select an insect they would like to research. On the practice paper they can write a descriptive poem about the insect.

2.   Cut a large brown paper bag so that it lies flat; place the print side down. Have the students draw a large insect shape on the paper bag.

3.   Use watercolor paint to color the image. Have the students cut out the shape and transfer the poem to the insect.

Florian, Douglas. *Insectlopedia.* San Diego: Harcourt Brace, 1998.

Jabuti the Tortoise: A Trickster Tale from the Amazon

Cut Paper Turtle

The artwork in the book uses bold colors. Students can use bright-colored construction paper to make a turtle.

Supplies

Bright-colored construction paper

Scissors

Glue

Pencil

Large circle pattern

Instructions

1. Using a pencil and a circle pattern, ask the students to draw a large circle on the construction paper.

2. Have them cut a variety of shapes to create a design on the turtle. Cut out small pieces for the turtle's legs, head, and tail.

McDermott, Gerald. *Jabuti the Tortoise: A Trickster Tale from the Amazon.* San Diego: Harcourt, 2001.

Gerald McDermott Website. URL: http://www.geraldmcdermott.com/ (Accessed March 26, 2002).

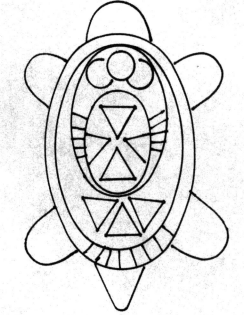

Jack's Black Book

Handmade Journal

The illustrations in this book look like they are pages from Jack's journal. Students can write and illustrate their own journals.

Supplies

See Part 1 for the supply list.

Instructions

1. Select one of the methods for constructing a book in chapter 1. Choose one of the techniques for decorating the cover.

2. Ask the students to write in their journals everyday.

Gantos, Jack. *Jack's Black Book.* New York: Farrar, Straus & Giroux, 1997.

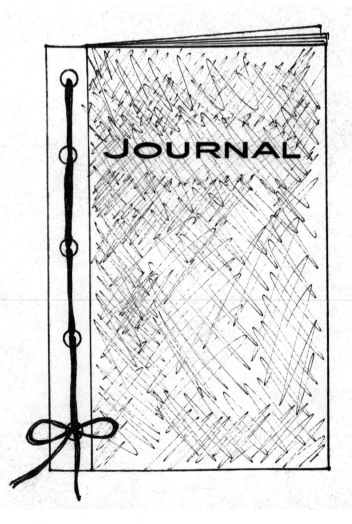

The Jolly Postman or Other People's Letters

Letters with Handmade Envelopes

The Jolly Postman goes on his route to deliver mail to fairy tale characters. Actual letters are tucked in the envelopes of this book. Students can use the template to create special envelopes to send their own letters to a fairy-tale character.

Supplies

Paper—wrapping paper, newspaper, magazines, or other papers

Photocopy of envelope pattern

Scissors

Pencil

Glue stick

Lined paper

Instructions

1. Have the students select the type of paper they would like to use. Trace the envelope pattern onto the back of the paper.

2. Cut out the envelope and glue it carefully with a glue stick.

3. Ask the students to select a fairy-tale character and write a letter.

Ahlberg, Janet and Allan Ahlberg. *The Jolly Postman or Other People's Letters.* Boston: Little, Brown, 1986.

The Journey

Side-Stitched Handmade Diary

An Amish girl writes in her diary about her first trip to the city. Students can write in a hand-made diary about a place they have visited.

Supplies

See page 10 for the supply list.

Instructions

1. Follow the instructions on page 10 for constructing a side-stitched book. Choose one of the techniques for decorating the cover.

2. Ask the students to write in their diaries daily.

Stewart, Sarah. *The Journey*. Illustrated by David Small. New York: Farrar, Straus & Giroux, 2001.

June 29, 1999

Collage

Holly sends vegetable seedlings into the sky for her school science project. On June 29, the sky fills with giant vegetables. Students can use collage to make an illustration of the giant vegetables.

Supplies

Magazines

Scissors

Glue

Paper

Instructions

1. Ask the students to search through magazines and find vegetable and landscape pictures to combine to create their own illustration.

2. Glue the pictures to a piece of background paper.

Wiesner, David. *June 29, 1999*. New York: Clarion Books, 1992.

Just the Way You Are

Hybrid Animal

Die cuts are used in this story to cleverly expose the silly hybrid creatures. Students can create their own creatures and use die cuts similar to the book.

Supplies

Paper

Pencil

Colored pencil

Instructions

1. Ask the students to create and name their own hybrid creature.

2. Once the creature is completed, ask the students to make a die-cut-style opening in a second paper that covers the drawing.

Pfister, Marcus. *Just the Way You Are*. New York: North South Books, 2002.

Kate and the Beanstalk

Tale with a New Character

This classic tale is retold with a girl in the role of Jack. Students can select a favorite tale to retell with a new character. Students can draw a picture of the new character.

Supplies

Lined practice paper

Lined paper

Drawing paper

Pencil

Instructions

1. Ask the students to select a classic tale they would like to rewrite with a new character. Ask them to begin with a rough draft on the lined practice paper.

2. Once they have a version they are happy with, they can transfer the finished writing to the lined paper.

3. Students can make an illustration of a character from their tale.

Osborne, Mary Pope. *Kate and the Beanstalk*. Illustrated by Giselle Potter. New York: Atheneum Books for Young Readers, 2000.

Katey's Dream List

My Dream List on Money Stationery

Katey finds $500 in Canadian money buried in the sand. The bank tells her that is equal to $440 United States money. Katey must wait 90 days to see if anyone claims the money. She makes a list of what she would buy if no one claims the money. Students can make their own list on money stationery.

Supplies

Photocopy machine

Pencil

Coins and paper money

Instructions

1. Have each student lay out a design on the photocopy machine using a variety of money. Have the students leave an open space in the center for writing their list.

2. Make a photocopy of the design.

3. Ask each student to make a list of how they would spend the money.

Fritz, T.J. *Katey's Dream List*. Pittsburgh, PA: Sterling House, 1999.

Sterling House Publisher's Website. URL: http://www.sterlinghousepublisher.com/ (Accessed March 26, 2002).

The Kissing Hand

Small Heart Envelope

Chester's mother sends him to school with a special way to carry her love. She kisses Chester's palm and tells him to put it to his cheek when he begins to feel lonely at school. Students can fold a small paper container to place a heart inside.

Supplies

Wrapping paper

Red construction paper

Pencil

Scissors

Envelope template

Instructions

1. Provide the students with a photocopy of the envelope template. Have the students trace the envelope pattern onto the back of the wrapping paper. Cut the envelope out and fold the shape.

2. Ask the students to cut a small heart from the red construction paper. Place the heart inside the envelope.

Penn, Audrey. *The Kissing Hand.* Illustrated by Ruth E. Harper and Nancy M. Leak. New York: Scholastic, 1998.

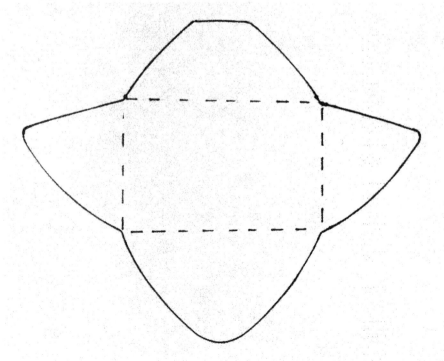

Lazy Daisy

Group Collage

Lazy Daisy has the messiest room in the world. Students can make a group collage using cutout shapes from catalogs showing the mess.

Supplies

Catalogs

Scissors

Glue

Bulletin Board

Instructions

1. Provide the students with an assortment of catalogs. Ask them to cut out pictures to help illustrate the mess in Lazy Daisy's room.

2. Attach the shapes to the bulletin board.

Olson, David. *Lazy Daisy*. Illustrated by Jenny Campbell. Nashville, TN: Ideals Childrens' Books, 2000.

The Legend of the Indian Paintbrush

Fake Buckskin Painting

This is a story of how the flower named the Indian paintbrush came to bloom in Texas. Students can paint a picture of a sunset on brown paper to give the appearance of a buckskin painting.

Supplies

Brown paper bags, brown paper towels, or brown package paper

Watercolor paints

Brushes

Glue

Twigs

Instructions

1. Provide each student with a piece of brown paper. Ask them to paint a sunset using watercolors.

2. When the painting is completely dry, have the students glue twigs around the outer edge.

DePaola, Tomie. *The Legend of the Indian Paintbrush*. New York: Putnam, 1988.

Little Wolf's Book of Badness

Letter from School

Little Wolf is sent away to his uncle's Big Bad Wolf School. He writes home to his parents about his experiences.

Supplies

Pencil

Practice paper

Lined paper

See page 26 for supplies for making envelopes.

Instructions

1. Have the students begin writing a letter about their school experiences on the practice paper.

2. They can transfer the finished letter to the lined paper.

3. Follow the instructions on page 26 for making an envelope.

Whybrow, Ian. *Little Wolf's Book of Badness*. Illustrated by Tony Ross. Minneapolis, MN: Carlrhoda Books, 1999.

Lizards, Frogs and Polliwogs

Amphibian or Reptile Painting and Report

This book contains a collection of funny poems about reptiles and amphibians. Students can make a watercolor painting similar to the artist's along with a report about a selected reptile or amphibian.

Supplies

Paper

Watercolor paint

Brushes

Water container

Writing paper

Instructions

1. Instruct the students to select an amphibian or reptile they want to research.

2. Once they have written a report, have the students paint a watercolor picture of the subject.

Florian, Douglas. *Lizards, Frogs and Polliwogs*. San Diego: Harcourt,. 2001.

The Lonely Scarecrow

Scarecrow

The lonely scarecrow has a scary face and has trouble making friends. When it snows and it covers the scarecrow, the animals are no longer afraid of him. Students can make their own scarecrow to place outside.

Supplies

Old clothing

Straw for stuffing

Large post

Burlap sack

Instructions

1. Construct one or more scarecrows in small groups.

2. Place the scarecrows outside near the classroom window.

Preston, Tim. *The Lonely Scarecrow*. Illustrated by Maggie Kneen. New York: Dutton Children's Books, 1999.

Look-Alikes

Group Assemblage

The author uses simple verse to give the reader clues to find everyday objects. The assemblage technique is used to make the scenes in the books. Assemblage uses objects to create a three-dimensional design. The design can be freestanding or mounted onto a flat surface. The elements added to an assemblage can be found objects or items made by the artist. Students can make a group assemblage.

Supplies

Found objects
Glue
Note cards
Pencil

Instructions

1. Divide the students into groups and let them decide what type of scene they want to create. Ask them to bring in the objects and begin construction.

2. Students can write clues using simple verse on note cards.

Steiner, Joan. *Look-alikes*. Photography by Thomas Lindley. Boston: Little, Brown, 1998.

Love Is...

Photograph

Students can select a line from the book and bring a photograph from home that expresses the line.

Supplies

Photographs

Paper

Pencil

Glue stick

Instructions

1. Ask the students to select a line from the poem and bring a photograph from home that is described by the line.

2. Students can attach the photograph to the paper. Ask them to write the line on the paper with the photograph.

Halperin, Wendy Anderson. *Love Is...* New York: Simon & Schuster Books for Young Readers, 2001.

Wendy Halperin Website. URL: http://www.wendyhalperin.com/ (Accessed March 26, 2002).

Love That Dog

Poetry Journal

Jack hates poetry and is very stubborn about his assignments. His teacher, Ms. Stretchberry, continues to give the poetry assignments and Jack finds that the more he writes, the more he has to say. The real life author, Walter Dean Myers, visits Jack in the story. Students can create a journal for writing their own poetry using a punch binding with fasteners.

Supplies

See page 8 for the supply list.

Instructions

Follow the instructions on page 8 for constructing a punch binding with fasteners.

Creech, Sharon. *Love That Dog*. New York: HarperCollins, 2001.

Sharon Creech Website. URL: http://www.sharoncreech.com/ (Accessed March 26, 2002).

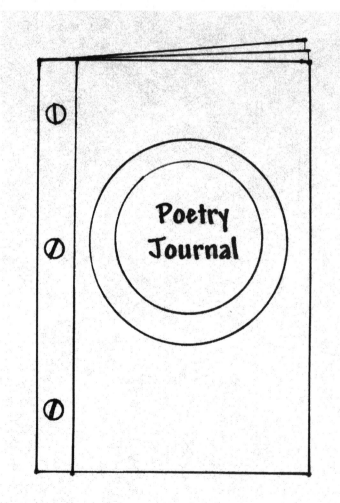

Lunch Money and Other Poems About School

School Poem with Illustration

This book contains a collection of school poems. Students can select a topic from their school day and write and illustrate a short poem about it.

Supplies

Practice paper

Lined paper

Drawing paper

Pencil

Instructions

1. Ask the students to write a poem about their school day on the practice paper. Once they have a version they are happy with, they can transfer the poem to the lined paper.

2. Have the students draw an illustration on the drawing paper.

Shields, Carol Diggory. *Lunch Money and Other Poems About School.* New York: Dutton Children's Books, 1995.

Make Up Mess

Self Portrait with Makeup

Julie buys $100 worth of makeup. After she applies it to her face, she finds that no one likes it. Students can make a self -portrait of how they would look if they bought $100 worth of makeup from Julie.

Supplies

Construction paper

Pencil

Scissors

Glue

Crayons

Instructions

1. Provide the students with construction paper to cut out a head with a neck and hair.

2. Ask the students to draw the eyes, nose, and mouth with pencil. Using crayons, the students can add makeup to their faces.

Munsch, Robert. *Make Up Mess*. Illustrated by Michael Martchenko. New York: Scholastic, 2001.

Robert Munsch Website. URL: http://www.robertmunsch.com/ (Accessed March 26, 2002).

Mammalabilia: Poems and Paintings

Stuffed Paper Sculpture

Students can research a mammal and write a short poem to go along with the stuffed paper sculpture.

Supplies

Two large sheets of drawing paper

Pencil

Acrylic or tempera paint

Brushes

Water container

Stapler

Scissors

Scrap paper for stuffing

Writing paper

Instructions

1. Ask the students to select a mammal they would like to research. Using pencil, have the students draw a large animal that fills the entire paper. Paint the entire image.

2. After the paint has dried, cut the shape out and trace the shape onto the second sheet of paper. Paint the outside surface of the paper and cut the shape out when dry.

3. Staple the two sheets of painted paper together leaving a small opening. Wad small pieces of scrap paper and stuff them into the opening. Staple the opening together.

4. Write a short poem that describes the mammal.

Florian, Douglas. *Mammalabilia*. San Diego: Harcourt, 2000.

Memory String

Polymer Clay Memory String

Memories are represented by 43 buttons on a string. Students can create their own memory string with polymer clay.

Supplies

Polymer clay

Carving tools

String

Instructions

1. Provide students with several colors of polymer clay. Have the students prepare the clay by kneading it with their hands.

2. Once the clay is soft, have the students roll the clay into small balls and poke holes into each ball.

3. Using the point of a carving tool, the students can carve important names and dates into the clay.

Bunting, Eve. *The Memory String*. Illustrated by Ted Rand. New York: Clarion Books, 2000.

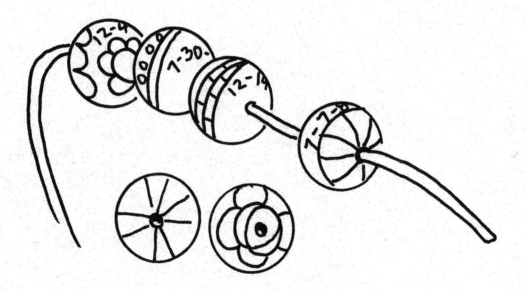

The Midnight Ride of Paul Revere/ Henry Wadsworth Longfellow; graved and painted by Christopher Bing

Wax Seal

The letters at the beginning and end of the story show the image of a wax seal. This was the method people used to close envelopes during Longfellow's time. Students can use polymer clay to make their own wax seals. The students can use the seals on a copy of the poem *The Midnight Ride of Paul Revere*.

Supplies

Polymer clay

Found objects to press into clay

Instructions

1.   First students will need to condition, or soften, the polymer clay by kneading it in their hands.

2.   Have the students roll a small ball of clay. Next, press the clay into a disk. Press an object into the clay to leave an image. Bake the clay according to the manufacturer's instructions.

3.   Attach the seal to a copy of the poem.

Bing, Christopher. *The Midnight Ride of Paul Revere / Henry Wadsworth Longfellow; graved and painted by Christopher Bing*. New York: Handprint Books, 2001.

Milo and the Magical Stones

Story with Two Endings

Halfway through the story, the book splits into two parts. Each part has a different ending, one happy and one sad. Students can write a different happy or sad ending for the story.

Supplies

Writing paper
Pencil

Instructions

1. Ask the students to select which ending they want to rewrite.

2. Have the students write their version of the story.

Pfister, Marcus. *Milo and the Magical Stones.* New York: North South Books, 1997.

Milo and the Magical Stones

Polymer Clay Stone

Milo carved a sun shape into a stone to give to the island in return for the beautiful stone he found. Students can make their own polymer clay stone.

Supplies

Polymer clay

Tools for carving

Instructions

1. Ask the students to soften the clay by kneading.

2. Have the students form the clay into a stone and carve a design.

3. Bake the clay according to the manufacturer's instructions.

Pfister, Marcus. *Milo and the Magical Stones.* New York: North South Books, 1997.

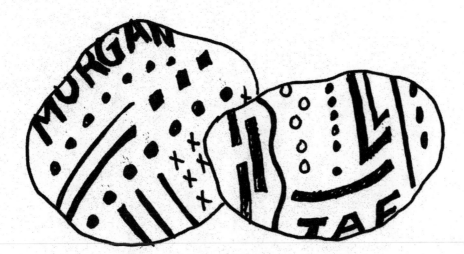

The Mitten: A Ukrainian Folktale

Paper Mitten

Students can make a paper mitten by tracing the shape of a real mitten. Color can be added with crayons.

Supplies

Drawing paper

Mitten

Crayons

Scissors

Yarn

Paper punch

Instructions

1. Ask the students to trace a pair of mittens on the sheet of drawing paper. Add a design to the mittens with crayons.

2. Cut the mitten out and punch a hole near the top and add the yarn.

Brett, Jan. *The Mitten: A Ukrainian Folktale*. New York: Putnam, 1989.

Jan Brett's Home Page. URL: http://www.janbrett.com/ (Accessed March 26, 2002).

Mmm, Cookies!

Clay Cookies

Students can make fake cookies using the play clay recipe.

Supplies

Clay recipe on page 16

Instructions

1. Follow the recipe for clay on page 16.

2. Provide students with a small ball of clay and ask them to make their own fake cookies.

Munsch, Robert. *Mmm, Cookies!* Illustrated by Michael Martchenko. New York: Scholastic, 2000.

Robert Munsch Website. URL: http://www.robertmunsch.com/ (Accessed March 26, 2002).

Monster Goose

Monster Nursery Rhymes and Illustration

The author has rewritten 25 nursery rhymes with a monster theme. Students can make their own monster nursery rhyme and an illustration.

Supplies

Pencil

Practice paper

Drawing paper

Instructions

1. Ask the students to select a nursery rhyme they would like to rewrite. Using the practice paper, they can write a rough draft.

2. Draw the monster version of the rhyme on the drawing paper. Transfer the rhyme to the bottom of the drawing.

Sierra, Judy. *Monster Goose*. Illustrated by Jack E. Davis. San Diego: Harcourt, 2001.

Mother Goose Remembers

Stitched Illustration

The illustrations in this book are hand sewn. Students can select a rhyme and make a simple stitched illustration.

Supplies

Scissors
Felt
Sewing needles
Thread

Instructions

1. Have the students select a nursery rhyme they would like to illustrate.

2. Cut the shapes out of the felt and follow the instructions on page 28 for stitching.

Beaton, Clare. *Mother Goose Remembers*. Cambridge, MA: Barefoot Books, 2000.

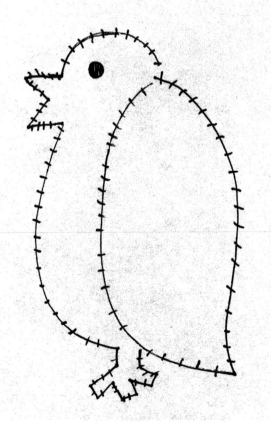

My Brother Made Me Do It

Senior Citizen Pen Pal

Julie Welsh writes letters to her 89-year-old pen pal. Student can have their own senior citizen pen pal to write letters to.

Supplies

Practice paper

Lined paper

Stamps

Envelope template

Assorted paper

Instructions

1. Contact a nursing home or senior center and get a list of senior citizens. Assign each student a pen pal.

2. Ask the students to write a draft of the letter introducing themselves to their pen pal. Transfer the letter to the good paper.

3. Follow the instructions on page 26 for making an envelope.

4. Have the students address their letters and mail them to their pen pals.

Kehret, Peg. *My Brother Made Me Do It*. New York: Pocket Books, 2000.

Peg Kehret Website. URL: http://www.pegkehret.com/ (Accessed March 26, 2002).

My Dad

Creating Imagery

Imagery is creating pictures in the reader's mind by using words to make the topic easier to understand or more interesting. In the book *My Dad*, a child describes all the great things about his dad. The author uses imagery: swims like a fish, soft as a teddy, and eats like a horse. The illustrations show what readers would picture in their minds using elements from *My Dad* to make their point. Students can write their own descriptions of their dads using imagery. One item can be selected to illustrate.

Supplies

Lined paper

Drawing paper

Pencil

Instructions

1.   Ask the students to create a list describing their dad. Use the words *is* and *like*.

2.   Ask the students to select one of the descriptions to illustrate. Make sure they include some element in their illustration that represents their dad such as glasses, favorite piece of clothing, or hairstyle.

Browne, Anthony. *My Dad*. New York: Farrar, Straus & Giroux, 2001.

My Nine Lives

A Pet's Journal

The book is a journal written by a cat. Students can write a journal from an animal's perspective.

Supplies

See the supplies on page 6 for an accordion book.

Instructions

1. Have the students follow the instructions on page 6 for making an accordion book.

2. Once the book is constructed, have the students write the events of daily life from the pet's point of view.

Clio. *My Nine Lives*. New York: Atheneum, 1998.

The Next Place

Paper Mosaic

The illustrations in this book use the mosaic technique. Traditional mosaic is the technique of placing small pieces of glass, stone, or ceramic in grout. It is one of the oldest forms of creating a picture. This project uses pieces of colored paper to create a similar effect.

Supplies

See the supply list on page 36 for making mosaics.

Instructions

1. Begin by lightly drawing the design on the background paper with pencil.

2. Follow the instructions on page 36 for making mosaics.

Hanson, Warren. *The Next Place*. Minneapolis, MN: Waldman House Press, 1999.

Warren Hanson Website. URL: http://www.warrenhanson.com/ (Accessed March 26, 2002).

No More Homework! No More Tests! Kids' Favorite Funny School Poems

Accordion-Style Poetry Book

This book is a collection of favorite school poems. Students can make an accordion book to collect their favorite funny school poems.

Supplies

Assortment of poetry books

Supply list from page 6

Instructions

1. Provide the students with an assortment of poetry books with school themes. Ask the students to select their favorite poems.

2. Follow the instructions on page 6 for making accordion books.

3. When the books are complete, have the students copy their favorite poems into their books.

Carpenter, Stephen. *No More Homework! No More Tests! Kids' Favorite Funny School Poems.* New York: Meadowbrook Press, 1997.

Once Upon a Fairy Tale: Four Favorite Stories/Retold by the Stars

Fairy Tale Retold

Four classic fairy tales are retold by 21 celebrities and 21 award-winning illustrators. Students can work in groups and retell a fairy tale.

Supplies

Assortment of books with fairy tales

Practice paper

Pencil

Lined paper

Drawing paper

Instructions

1. Divide the students into small groups. Ask them to select a fairy tale.

2. Divide the story into parts and have each member of the group rewrite and illustrate his or her section of the tale.

Once Upon a Fairy Tale: Four Favorite Stories/Retold by the Stars. New York: Viking, 2001.

100th Day Worries

100 Objects Bulletin Board

Jessica worries about what to bring for the 100th day of school. Students can put themselves in Jessica's position and select a theme for 100 objects to bring to school. Provide each student with the same size plastic bag to place objects in for displaying on the bulletin board.

Supplies

100 objects

Plastic bags

Instructions

1. Ask the students to select a theme for 100 items. All the items must fit in the plastic bag.

2. Hang all the bags together on the bulletin board.

Cuyler, Margery. *100th Day Worries*. Illustrated by Arthur Howard, New York: Simon & Schuster Books for Young Readers, 2000.

Peepers

Leaf Prints

The illustrations in this book show the colors of fall. Students can collect leaves to make leaf prints.

Supplies

Assorted leaves

Acrylic paint

Paint brushes

White paper

Scrap paper

Instructions

1.   Ask the students to bring in a variety of leaves. Place the leaves on a piece of scrap paper and coat the surface with paint.

2.   Place the coated leaf on the white paper, paint-side down. Place a piece of scrap paper over top of the leaf and rub to transfer the paint. Repeat the process with a variety of shapes, sizes, and colors.

Bunting, Eve. *Peepers*. Illustrated by James Ransome. San Diego: Harcourt Brace & Company, 2000.

Piggies

Drawing

The illustrations of the pigs in the story show the adjectives the author uses to describe each pig. Students can illustrate an adjective with a drawing of a pig.

Supplies

Drawing paper

Pencil

Colored pencil

Instructions

1. First, have the students trace their hand on the drawing paper.

2. Have the students select an adjective.

3. Using a pencil, have the students draw their pig on one of the fingers illustrating the adjective.

4. Add color to the drawing using colored pencils.

Wood, Audrey and Don Wood. *Piggies.* San Diego: Harcourt, 1996.

Audrey Wood Clubhouse. URL: http://www.audreywood.com/ (Accessed March 26, 2002).

A Poke in the I: A Collection of Concrete Poems

Creating Concrete Poems

In concrete poems, the way the letters or words are arranged on the page, the font that is chosen, and the way the space is used adds meaning to the poem beyond what is contained in the actual words. Students can create their own concrete poems.

Supplies

Practice paper

Drawing paper

Pencil

Instructions

1. Examine the book with the class. Look at how the concrete poems work.

2. Have the students begin by making a list of possible topics. Then, on the practice paper ask the students to begin drawing their ideas.

3. Transfer the final design to the drawing paper.

Janeczko, Paul B. *A Poke in the I: A Collection of Concrete Poems*. Illustrated by Chris Raschka. Cambridge, MA: Candlewick Press, 2001.

The Potter Giselle

Polymer Clay Pot

Giselle the potter is ordered to make a magnificent pot for King Orville, but his brother, King Ludlow, insists that she make an even bigger one for him. Students can make their own pot using polymer clay.

Supplies

Polymer clay

Instructions

1.   Provide each student with a ball of clay. Have them soften the clay by kneading it in their hands.

2.   Using their fingers, ask the students to form a small pot. Follow the manufacturer's instructions for baking the clay.

Aarestad, Thomas. *The Potter Giselle*. Nashville, TN: Ideals Childrens' Books, 1999.

Purple, Green, and Yellow

Self Portrait with Markers

Brigid uses her body as a painting canvas. Students can make a self-portrait of how they would look if they used the markers like Brigid.

Supplies

Large drawing paper
Pencil
Assorted markers

Instructions

1. Ask the students to draw a large self-portrait on the drawing paper using pencil.

2. Add a design to the figure using the markers.

Munsch, Robert. *Purple, Green, and Yellow*. Illustrated by Helene Desputeaux. New York: Annick Press, 1992.

Robert Munsch Website. URL: http://www.robertmunsch.com/ (Accessed March 26, 2002).

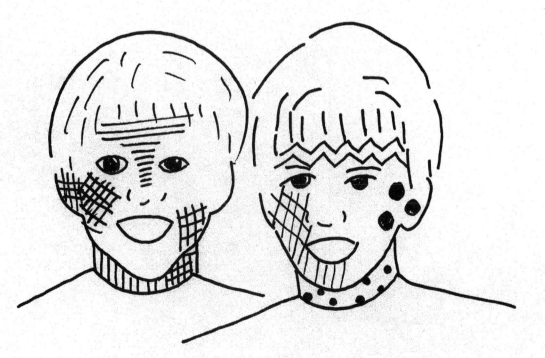

Quilt Alphabet

Quilt Block with Clue

Every letter of the alphabet has a poem and a rhyming clue. The letter is placed inside a quilt block. Students can create their own quilt block and rhyming clue.

Supplies

Paper
Pencil
Crayons
Rulers

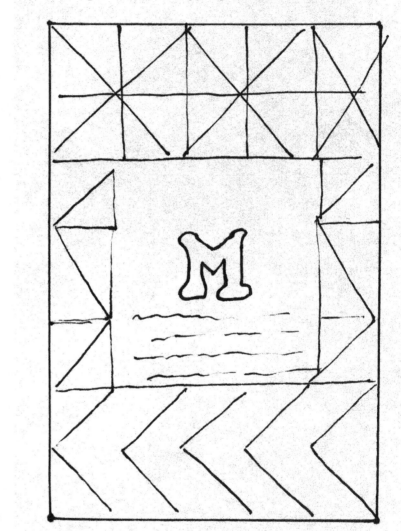

Instructions

1. Assign each student a letter of the alphabet. Ask the students to select an object that begins with that letter.

2. Have the students write a rhyming clue that describes the object they selected.

3. Have the students draw the letter on the paper and use a ruler to create a quilt block design.

4. Have the students write their clues on the design.

Ransome, Lesa Cline. *Quilt Alphabet.* New York: Holiday House, 2001.

Quilt of Dreams

Quilt Design Bookmark

Katy and her mother finish a quilt started by her grandmother before she died. Students can select one of the patterns in the book to make a quilt bookmark.

Supplies

Cover stock
Ruler
Pencil
Colored pencils
Paper punch
Ribbon

Instructions

1. Ask the students to select a pattern they would like to draw on the bookmark.

2. Have the students begin by drawing the pattern using pencil and ruler, then add color to the design with the colored pencils.

3. Punch a hole in the top of the design and add the ribbon.

Dwyer, Mindy. *Quilt of Dreams*. Portland, OR: Alaska Northwest Books, 2000.

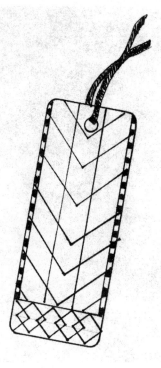

The Quiltmaker's Gift

Sandpaper Print Group Quilt

A quilt maker agrees to make a quilt for a greedy king and causes him to undergo a change of heart. Using the sandpaper printing method, students can make an individual block for a fabric quilt. Students can create a design on a piece of sandpaper with crayon. When heated, the design can be transferred to the fabric.

Supplies

See the supply list on page 20

Practice drawing paper

Pencil

Fabric

Instructions

1. Show the students samples of quilts. Have them draw a quilt design onto a practice paper. Draw the design in crayon on the sandpaper, pressing heavily.

2. Have a piece of fabric large enough to fit all the students' work.

3. Follow the instructions on page 20 for making a sandpaper print.

Brumbeau, Jeff. *The Quiltmaker's Gift*. New York: Scholastic, 2000.

Quiltmaker's Gift Website. URL: http://www.quiltmakersgift.com/index.htm (Accessed March 26, 2002).

Rachel Field's Hitty: Her First Hundred Years

Toy with Journal

The doll goes on many adventures with various owners. Students can send a class doll or stuffed animal on adventures by sending the toy home with each student in the class. Send a journal along so the students can write their activities in the journal.

Supplies

Stuffed animal or doll

Notebook or journal

Instructions

1. Take turns sending a selected toy home over the weekend with each student in the class.

2. Have the students and parents write a page about the weekend the toy spent with the family.

Wells, Rosemary, and Susan Jeffers. *Rachel Field's Hitty: Her First Hundred Years*. New York: Simon & Schuster Books for Young Readers, 1999.

The World of Rosemary Wells. URL: http://www.rosemarywells.com/ (Accessed March 26, 2002).

Rachel Field's Hitty: Her First Hundred Years

Map with Descriptions

The map shows the different places Hitty traveled. Using a photocopy of a map, students can plot out locations of places they have traveled. Students can include a brief description about each place.

Supplies

Photocopies of maps
Small star stickers
White paper
Glue sticks

Instructions

1.   Provide each student with a photocopy of a map. Using the small star stickers, have the students mark the locations of the places they have visited.

2.   Ask the students to cut small labels from the white paper and write a brief description of each location. Glue the labels near the stars.

Wells, Rosemary and Susan Jeffers. *Rachel Field's Hitty: Her First Hundred Years*. New York: Simon & Schuster Books for Young Readers, 1999.

The World of Rosemary Wells. URL: http://www.rosemarywells.com/ (Accessed March 26, 2002).

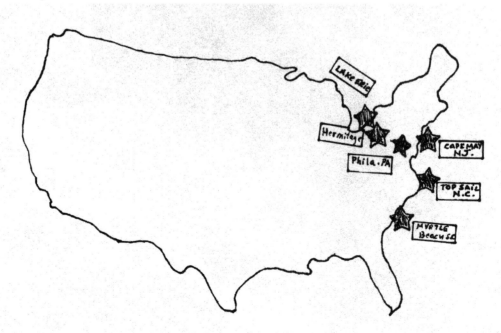

Raven: A Trickster Tale from the Pacific Northwest

Construction Paper Raven

The raven is a symbol in many Native American stories. Students can use construction paper to make a raven.

Supplies

Assorted construction paper

Scissors

Glue

Pencil

Instructions

1. Ask the students to begin by drawing the raven's shape lightly with pencil. Cut out the shape.

2. Next, ask the students to cut shapes out of the construction paper to decorate the raven.

McDermott, Gerald. *Raven.* New York: Scholastic, 1993.

Gerald McDermott Website. URL: http://www.geraldmcdermott.com/ (Accessed March 26, 2002).

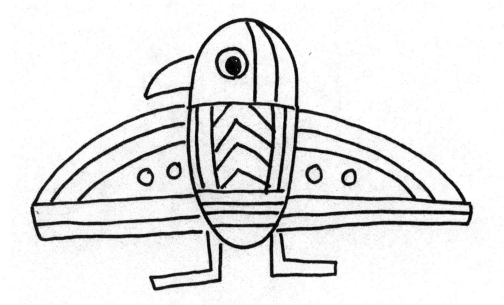

Rechenka's Eggs

Egg Design

Students can make their own decorated eggs like Babushka in the story.

Supplies

White crayons
Eggs
Dyes

Instructions

1. Begin with hardboiled eggs. Ask the students to draw a design on the egg using the white crayon.

2. Once the design is complete, have the students dip the egg in dye. The dye will not adhere to the egg where there is crayon.

Polacco, Patricia. *Rechenka's Eggs*. New York: Philomel Books, 1988.

Red Leaf, Yellow Leaf

Paper Leaves

This book describes the growth of a maple tree from seed to sapling. Students can make their own leaves similar to the ones in the illustrations by crumpling painted paper and rubbing the paper with crayons.

Supplies

Crayons

Lightweight paper

Watercolor paints

Brushes

Scissors

Instructions

1. Have the students begin by covering the entire paper with assorted colors of thinned paint.

2. Once the paint is dry, ask the students to crumple the paper into a ball. Flatten the paper and rub using the side of a peeled crayon.

3. Cut the paper into the shape of leaves.

Ehlert, Lois. *Red Leaf, Yellow Leaf.* San Diego: Harcourt Brace Jovano

Remember the Ladies: 100 Great American Women

American Women Bulletin Board

This book contains the profiles of 100 notable American women arranged in chronological order. Students can create a bulletin board using the same technique.

Supplies

Paper

Pencil

Colored pencils

Instructions

1.   Ask the students to select a famous American woman to research.

2.   Students can write a description and draw an illustration.

3.   Place the work on a bulletin board in chronological order.

Harness, Cheryl. *Remember the Ladies: 100 Great American Women.* New York: HarperCollins, 2001.

The Reptile Room

Snake Drawing with Misnomer Name

Uncle Monty named the snake he discovered "the Incredibly Deadly Viper." This name is a misnomer, a wrong meaning. Students can draw a snake of their own and give it a name that is a misnomer.

Supplies

Drawing paper

Pencil

Markers or colored pencils

Instructions

1. Have the students draw a picture of a snake. They can use colored pencils or markers to add color.

2. Ask the students to give the snake a name that is a misnomer.

Snicket, Lemony. *The Reptile Room.* Illustrated by Brett Helquist. New York: HarperCollins, 1999.

The Lemony Snicket Website. URL: http://www.lemonysnicket.com/ (Accessed March 26, 2002).

The Reptile Room

Snake Report with Paper Snake

Students can select a snake they would like to research. Have the students make a paper snake using the paper sculpture technique on page 38.

Supplies

Pencil

Writing paper

Rope

Supplies for paper sculpture on page 38

Instructions

1. Ask the students to select a snake they would like to research. They can write a report about the snake.

2. Following the instructions on page 38, students can make a paper sculpture snake. Use a piece of rope for the base shape to cover with the paper and glue.

Snicket, Lemony. *The Reptile Room.* Illustrated by Brett Helquist. New York: HarperCollins, 1999.

The Lemony Snicket Website. URL: http://www.lemonysnicket.com/ (Accessed March 26, 2002).

Sally Goes to the Mountains

Potato Print

This is a story of Sally, a black Labrador. The artist used woodcut prints in the illustrations. Students can carve a design into a potato to create the same type of image.

Supplies

Large potatoes

Plastic knives

Acrylic paint

Brush

Paper

Instructions

1. Provide the students with half of a large potato. Ask the students to carve a design into the potato using plastic knives.

2. Coat the carved potato with paint and stamp in onto the paper.

Huneck, Stephen. *Sally Goes to the Mountains*. New York: Harry N. Abrams, 2001.

Stephen Huneck Gallery. URL: http://www.huneck.com/ (Accessed March 26, 2002).

Scarecrow

Construction Paper Scarecrow

Students can make their own scarecrows using construction paper.

Supplies

Construction paper

Scissors

Glue

Straw pieces

Instructions

1. Provide students with a variety of construction paper.

2. Have the students cut out and assemble their scarecrows.

Rylant, Cynthia. *Scarecrow*. Illustrated by Lauren Stringer. San Diego: Harcourt Brace, 1998.

The Secret Knowledge of Grown-ups

Computer Design

This book takes a look at the rules kids have to follow and provides the reader with the humorous reasons these rules exist. The computer can be used to create the art. Have the students make their own files.

Supplies

Computer with a word-processing program

Printer

Paper

File folders

Glue

Scissors

Instructions

1. Ask the students to select a rule.

2. Next, ask the students to type their file and include the following information: Grown up rule # __, Official Reason, and The Truth.

3. Print the information onto a sheet of paper. Place the paper in a file folder.

4. Type words like "top secret," "classified," and "private" to decorate the outside of the file. Change the font style, size, and color. Cut the words apart and paste them to the file.

Wisniewski, David. *The Secret Knowledge of Grown-ups*. New York: HarperCollins, 1998.

The Secret to Freedom

Photocopy on Fabric

Great Aunt Lucy tells the story of how she learned the quilt code to help direct slaves to freedom. The book contains patterns and their meanings. Students can select one of the patterns to write and illustrate.

Supplies

Graph paper

Pencil

Black fine-point marker

Colored pencils

See the supply list on page 42 for photocopying on fabric.

Lined paper

Instructions

1. Students can select one of the quilt patterns to draw on the graph paper with pencil. Have the students draw on top of the pencil lines with a black fine-point marker.

2. Follow the instructions on page 42 for making a photocopy on fabric. Once the image is complete, have the students add color to the fabric design.

3. Students can include a paragraph with a description of the pattern's meaning.

Vaughan, Marcia. *The Secret to Freedom*. Illustrated by Larry Johnson. New York: Lee & Low Books, 2001.

Six Sick Sheep, 101 Tongue Twisters

Tongue Twister with Illustration

This is a collection of tongue twisters. Students can write and illustrate their own tongue twister.

Supplies

Paper

Pencil

Instructions

1. Ask the students to begin by selecting a topic for their tongue twister. Using words beginning with the same letter, ask them to create their tongue twister.

2. Students can make an illustration to go along with their tongue twister.

Cole, Joanna and Stephanie Calmenson. *Six Sick Sheep, 101 Tongue Twisters*. Illustrated by Alan Tiegreen. New York: Beech Tree Paperback Book, 1993.

The 6th Grade Nickname Game

Nicknames

Jeff and Wiley have given almost the entire school nicknames. Students can invent nicknames for all of their acquaintances that describe their personalities. Photographs can be taken that show the personality.

Supplies

Lined paper

Pencil

Camera

Film

Instructions

1. Have the students begin by making a list of people. Next, write all the characteristics they can think of for each person. Have the students create the nicknames.

2. Have the students photograph the people and show the personality in the picture. Polaroid cameras can be used if an instant picture is desired.

Korman, Gordon. *The 6th Grade Nickname Game*. New York: Hyperion Books for Children, 1998.

Smoky Night

Group Assemblage

The author uses assemblage to illustrate the story of the Los Angles riots. Assemblage is an art technique that uses objects to create a three-dimensional design. The design can be freestanding or mounted onto a flat surface. The elements added to an assemblage can be found objects or items made by the artist. Drawing, painting, and stamping can also be added to the design. Students can make a group assemblage.

Supplies

Glue

Found objects

Large picture frame

Instructions

1. Select a theme and have the students bring in a variety of objects.

2. Instruct the students to take turns gluing the objects inside the frame to create the design.

Bunting, Eve. *Smoky Night.* Illustrated by David Diaz. San Diego: Harcourt Brace, 1994.

1995 Caldecott Medal Winner

Snowflake Bentley

Nature Photographs

W.A. Bentley photographed nature up close. His photographs show the viewer the parts of nature that they might never notice. Students can use a Polaroid camera to take close-up photographs of nature.

Supplies

Polaroid camera

Instructions

Provide students with a Polaroid camera to photograph nature up close.

Martin, Jacqueline Briggs. *Snowflake Bentley*. Illustrated by Mary Azarian. Boston: Houghton Mifflin, 1998.

Jacqueline Briggs Martin Web Page. URL: http://www.jacquelinebriggsmartin.com/ (Accessed March 26, 2002).

1999 Caldecott Medal Winner

Sophie's Masterpiece: A Spider's Tale

Spider Web

Sophie the spider makes beautiful webs. Students can make their own spider webs with white crayon on black paper.

Supplies

White crayon

Black paper

Ruler

Pencil

Instructions

1. Using a pencil, have the students lightly draw a web design on the black paper. Remind the students that eraser marks on the black paper will show.

2. Use crayons to draw over the top of the pencil lines.

Spinelli, Eileen. *Sophie's Masterpiece: A Spider's Tale*. Illustrated by Jane Dyer. New York: Simon & Schuster Books for Young Readers, 2001.

Squids Will be Squids: Fresh Morals, Beastly Fables

Contemporary Fables

Students can select a fable to retell and illustrate using a modern theme.

Supplies

Books with fables
Practice paper
Pencil
White drawing paper
Lined paper

Instructions

1. Ask the students to select a fable they would like to retell. Use the practice paper to write a rough draft and sketch the illustration.

2. Students can write their final draft onto the lined paper and draw their final illustration on the white drawing paper.

Scieszka, John. *Squids Will be Squids: Fresh Morals, Beastly Fables*. Illustrated by Lane Smith. New York: Viking, 1998.

Stranger in the Woods

Snowman

Students can build their own snowman and watch to see what animals will visit. They can attract birds, squirrels, and deer by placing food nearby. Students can photograph the visitors.

Supplies

Accessories for making a snowman

Animal food

Polaroid camera

Instructions

1. Have the students build one or more snowmen close to the classroom window. Use accessories to decorate the snowman.

2. Place food near the snowmen to attract animals. Photograph any visitors that stop to eat.

Sams, Carl R. and Jean Stoick. *Stranger in the Woods: A Photographic Fantasy*. Milford, MI: C.R. Sams II Photography, 2000.

Stranger in the Woods Website. URL: http://www.strangerinthewoods.com/ (Accessed March 26, 2002).

Stringbean's Trip to the Shining Sea: Greetings from Vera B. Williams

Postcard Design

Stringbean describes his trip to the West Coast in a series of postcards. Students can make their own postcards to describe a place they have visited.

Supplies

Cover stock

Pencils

Practice paper

Colored pencils

Instructions

1. Cut the cover stock to approximately 4" x 6". Ask the students to use the practice paper and sketch out a picture for the front of their cards. They can write a descriptive note to a person on the practice paper.

2. Have the students draw the picture on the card stock and write the final draft of their note on the backs of the postcards.

3. Instruct the students on the proper technique for addressing the postcard. Fake postage can be added; see the instructions on page 2.

Williams, Vera B. *Stringbean's Trip to the Shining Sea: Greetings from Vera B. Williams*. Illustrated by Jennifer Williams. New York: Greenwillow Books, 1988.

Sweet Dream Pie

Wild Dream Creature

Ma Brindle makes Sweet Dream Pie for the whole neighborhood. Too much sweetness causes a restless night and wild dreams. Students can make a wild dream creature using bright-colored construction paper. Students can write a description of a wild dream.

Supplies

Assorted construction paper

Scissors

Glue

Pencil

Writing paper

Instructions

1. Ask the students to look at the creatures in the book illustration of the wild dreams. The students can create their own version using an assortment of colored construction paper.

2. Ask the students to write a description of a wild dream.

Wood, Audrey. *Sweet Dream Pie*. Illustrated by Mark Teague. New York: Blue Sky Press. 1998.

The Audrey Wood Clubhouse. URL: http://www.audreywood.com/ (Accessed March 26, 2002).

Swimmy

Underwater Scene with Stamped Fish

Crumpled paper can be used as a painting tool to create a background that is similar to the water scenes in *Swimmy*. A sponge cut into a fish shape can be used to stamp small red fish onto the design.

Supplies

Acrylic or tempera paints

White paper

Crumpled paper

Pressed sponge

Scissors

Instructions

1. Have the students begin by creating the background. Dip crumpled paper into blue paint and stamp the paint onto the white paper.

2. Once the entire background is covered, the students can stamp the fish with the shape they cut from the pressed sponge.

Lionni, Leo. *Swimmy*. New York: Scholastic, 1989.

Table Manners

Placemat with Manners

This how-to book gives information on topics including eating with your mouth closed, chewing properly, and using napkins. Students can make a placemat with reminders for proper manners.

Supplies

Large drawing paper

Pencils

Crayons

Instructions

1.   Provide the students with a sheet of drawing paper the size of a placemat.

2.   Have them decorate the paper with pictures and rules for proper manners.

Raschka, Chris and Vladimir Radunsky. *Table Manners*. Cambridge, MA: Candlewick Press, 2001.

Take Me Out to the Bathtub and Other Silly Dilly Songs

Silly Song and Illustration

Well-known songs are presented in this book with new words. Students can select a well-known song to illustrate and rewrite with new words.

Supplies

Drawing paper

Lined paper

Pencil

Colored pencils

Instructions

1. Ask the students to select a song and write the changes.

2. Using colored pencils, have the students draw an illustration to go with the changes to the song.

Katz, Alan. *Take Me Out to the Bathtub and Other Silly Dilly Songs.* Illustrated by David Catron. New York: Margaret McEldery Books, 2001.

The Talking Cloth

Photocopy on Fabric

Amber learns the significance of the colors and symbols in Aunt Phoebe's cloth. Students can design a cloth using some of the same symbols.

Supplies

Photocopy paper

Supplies on page 42 for making a photocopy on fabric

Instructions

1. Have the students draw a design with pencil on the photocopy paper and then go over the design with black marker.

2. Follow the instructions on page 42 for making a photocopy on fabric.

Mitchell, Rhonda. *The Talking Cloth*. New York: Orchard Books, 1997.

Tar Beach

Quilt Border Picture Frame

The artwork in this book has a quilt border. Students can use small pieces of fabric to create a quilt border picture frame.

Supplies

Assorted fabric scraps

Scissors

Glue

Cardboard frame or mat

Instructions

1. Ask the students to cut scrap fabric into small shapes.

2. Glue the shapes onto the surface of a cardboard frame or mat in a quilt pattern. The fabric should wrap around the edges.

Ringgold, Faith. *Tar Beach*. New York: Crown Publication, 1991.

Faith Ringgold Website. URL: http://www.faithringgold.com/ (Accessed March 26, 2002).

1992 Coretta Scott King Illustrator Award Winner

There Was an Old Lady Who Swallowed a Fly

Bulletin Board Design

This story is a traditional cumulative rhyme. Students can create a group bulletin board and their own rhyme.

Supplies

Construction paper

Scissors

Glue

Paper

Instructions

1. Begin by having the class construct its version of the old lady. Place the figure on the bulletin board.

2. Once the figure is complete, work with the class to compose the rhyme using something other than a fly.

3. Use construction paper to make shapes and attach them to the old lady's stomach.

Taback, Simms. *There Was an Old Lady Who Swallowed a Fly.* New York: Viking, 1997.

There's a Cow in the Cabbage Patch

Fabric Appliqué Animals

The animals on this farm are out of place until it is time for dinner. The artwork is made with fabrics, braids, buttons, and beads. Appliqué is a method of applying a decoration to the surface of fabric. The decoration is typically made from fabric and stitched into place. Students can make an appliquéd design.

Supplies

Drawing paper

Pencil

Assorted pieces of felt

Scissors

Needles

Thread

Buttons and beads

Instructions

1. Have the students draw a simple animal shape on the drawing paper. Draw that shape onto the felt with pencil and cut out the shape.

2. Place the animal shape onto a larger piece of felt and stitch the shape with thread. See page 28 for basic stitches. Add other items such as buttons and beads for decorations.

Beaton, Clare. *There's a Cow in the Cabbage Patch*. Cambridge, MA: Barefoot Books, 2001.

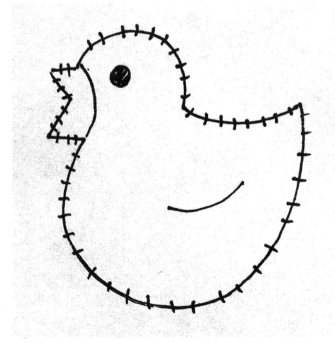

The 13 Nights of Halloween

Spooky Gifts

This is the Halloween version of the 12 Days of Christmas. Students can select one of the nights of Halloween to create their own spooky gifts.

Supplies

Construction paper

Pencil

Glue

Scissors

Instructions

1. Ask the students to select one of the nights of Halloween to create a spooky gift.

2. Use construction paper to create the gifts.

Dickinson, Rebecca. *The 13 Nights of Halloween*. New York: Scholastic. 1996.

Things That Are Most in the World

Superlative Collage

Students can combine images found in magazines with drawings to create their own superlatives.

Supplies

Practice paper

Magazines

Pencils

Glue

Scissors

Drawing paper

Instructions

1. Ask the students to write a list of superlatives on the practice paper.

2. Next, find images in the magazines and combine them with drawings to illustrate each superlative.

Barrett, Judi. *Things That Are Most in the World*. Illustrated by John Nickle. New York: Aladdin, 2001.

Time Stops for No Mouse

Watch Design

Watchmaker Hermux Tantamoq's adventure begins when Ms. Perflinger drops off a watch for him to fix. Students can create their own version of how they think the watch looked.

Supplies

Construction paper

Pencil

Glue

Scissors

Instructions

Have the students create an image of a watch using construction paper.

Hoeye, Michael. *Time Stops for No Mouse*. New York: G.P. Putnam's Sons, 2002.

Today I Feel Silly & Other Moods That Make My Day

Face with Changing Moods

By using a wheel that turns, students can create a face that changes expressions to show different moods.

Supplies

Circle pattern

Two sheets of paper

Prong fasteners

Crayons

Pencils

Scissors

Instructions

1. Have the students begin with two identical circles. Join them together in the center with the prong fastener. The prong will also serve as the nose.

2. Draw eyes on the circle. Add any additional features on the face except the mouth.

3. Once the design is complete, have the students cut an opening in the top circle where the mouth should be. Have them draw several different types of mouths on the bottom circle, through the opening.

Curtis, Jamie Lee. *Today I Feel Silly & Other Moods That Make My Day*. Illustrated by Laura Cornell. New York: HarperCollins, 1998.

HarperCollins Children's Website. URL: http://www.harperchildrens.com/hch/ (Accessed March 26, 2002).

To Market, To Market

New Version with a Drawing

This book starts with the nursery rhyme *To Market, To Market* and then the story changes. Students can make their own changes to the nursery rhyme.

Supplies

Pencils

Practice paper

Drawing paper

Instructions

1. Begin by reading the original rhyme to the students, and then read Anne Miranda's version.

2. Ask the students to make their changes to the rhyme along with an illustration.

Miranda, Anne. *To Market, To Market.* Illustrated by Janet Stevens. San Diego: Voyager Books, 2001.

Tops & Bottoms

Decorative Pots for Planting

Students can use acrylic paints to decorate terra-cotta pots. The pots can be used to plant a variety of vegetables.

Supplies

Terra-cotta pots

Acrylic paint

Brushes

Water

Seeds

Potting soil

Instructions

1. Using acrylic paints, have the students decorate the outside of the clay pots.

2. Once the paints have dried, plant a variety of seeds in the pots. Select seeds that will produce vegetables with edible tops or bottoms.

Stevens, Janet. *Tops & Bottoms*. San Diego: Harcourt Brace, 1995.

Janet Stevens Website. URL: http://www.janetstevens.com/ (Accessed March 26, 2002).

The True Story of the 3 Little Pigs

My Version of the Three Little Pigs

The *Three Little Pigs* is a popular story. There are many books that have used the basic story and changed aspects of the story to give it a twist. Students can rewrite the story to give it a new twist.

Supplies

Practice paper

Lined paper

Pencil

White paper

Instructions

1. Read several versions of *The Three Little Pigs* to the class. Let the students write their own version on the practice paper, then transfer the final draft to the lined paper.

2. Students can draw an illustration to go along with the story.

Scieszka, Jon. *The True Story of the 3 Little Pigs*. Illustrated by Lane Smith. New York: Viking, 1999.

Uptown

Collage of Your Community

The illustrations in this book take the viewer on a tour of Harlem. The artist uses collage to make the landmarks throughout the city. Students can use collage to make a landmark from their community.

Supplies

Magazines

Paper

Scissors

Glue

Writing paper

Instructions

1. Divide the students into groups. Have them select a local landmark.

2. Ask the students to find images in magazines to construct a picture of the landmark.

3. Students can then write a description about the landmark.

Collier, Bryan. *Uptown.* New York: Henry Holt, 2000.

Bryan Collier Website. URL: http://www.bryancollier.com/ (Accessed March 26, 2002).

2001 Coretta Scott King Illustrators Award Winner

Visiting Langston

Report with Collage

This book is a poem that honors Langston Hughes, an African American poet. The book begins with a brief report about Hughes. The artwork is collage. Students can write a report about a famous person they admire and combine the report with a collage image.

Supplies

Practice paper

Pencil

Lined paper

Drawing paper

Collage papers

Scissors

Glue

Instructions

1. Have the students select a person they would like to do a report about. Use the practice paper to write a rough draft.

2. Ask the students to make a drawing of the person in their report. Combine other papers with the drawing to create the collage.

Perdomo, Willie. *Visiting Langston*. Illustrated by Bryan Collier. New York: Henry Holt, 2002.

The Academy of American Poets Website. URL: http://www.poets.org/poets/index.cfm (Accessed March 26, 2002).

Waiting for Wings

Dyed Butterfly Design and Journal

This book uses beautiful artwork to show how a butterfly transforms from an egg to new butterfly. Students can create butterflies similar to the artist's using a simple dye technique. The butterflies can be used to decorate the outside of a handmade notebook that the students can use to write down their observations of a butterfly.

Supplies

Coffee filters

Bowl of water

Acrylic paints

Paper towels

Glue

Scissors

Supplies on page 10 for making side-stitched books

Instructions

1. Prepare the paint by mixing four to five drops of liquid acrylic paint in a bowl of water.

2. Provide several coffee filters for each student. Ask them to explore different methods of folding and dipping the filters into the watered-down paint.

3. Once the coffee filters are dry, they can be cut into butterflies. Scraps from the extra filters can be cut and glued onto the butterflies.

4. Follow the instructions on page 10 for making a side-stitched book. Glue the butterfly to the front cover.

Ehlert, Lois. *Waiting for Wings*. San Diego: Harcourt, 2001.

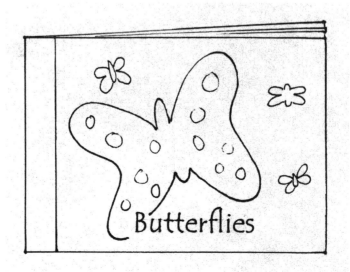

What Do Ducks Dream?

Dream Drawing

The animals and human inhabitants of Sigmund's farm have a variety of nighttime dreams. Have the students draw a picture of a dream and write a description.

Supplies

Drawing paper
Pencil
Colored pencils
Lined paper

Instructions

Ask the students to draw a picture of a dream and write a description.

Ziefert, Harriet. *What Do Ducks Dream?* Illustrated by Donald Saaf. New York: G.P. Putnam's
   Sons, 2001.

What Planet Are You From, Clarice Bean?

Nature Observation Book

The text in this story is not presented in traditional straight lines. The words move around the pages and are placed on different parts of the illustrations. Students can make a simple accordion book to write their observations about the environment. The students can combine collage and free-form writing similar to the book.

Supplies

Supplies from page 6

Pencil

Paper for collage

Glue

Instructions

1.   Follow the instructions on page 6 for making an accordion book.

2.   Students can make a collage and also write their observations about the environment.

Child, Lauren. *What Planet Are You From, Clarice Bean?* Cambridge, MA: Candlewick Press, 2001.

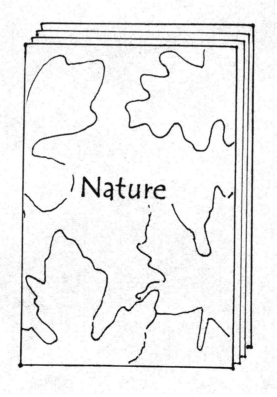

When the Wind Stops

Sun Wood Painting

The illustrations in this book are paintings on wood. Students can make a sun painting on wood.

Supplies

Blocks of wood
Watercolor paints
Brushes
Pencils

Instructions

1. Have the students draw a picture of a sun on the wood block with pencil.

2. Using watercolor paint, have the students add color to their design.

Zolotow, Charlotte. *When the Wind Stops*. Illustrated by Stefano Vitale. New York: HarperCollins, 1995.

Charlotte Zolotow Website. URL:http://www.charlottezolotow.com/ (Accessed March 26, 2002).

Where the Sidewalk Ends

I Cannot Go to School Today

The poem "Sick" lists all the reasons why Peggy Ann McKay cannot go to school. Students can make their own rhyming poem listing all the reasons they cannot go to school.

Supplies

Practice writing paper

Writing paper

Pencil

Instructions

1. Have the students begin by listing all the excuses they can come up with for why they cannot go to school.

2. Have the students put the reasons into a rhyming poem and transfer to the lined paper.

Silverstein, Shel. *Where the Sidewalk Ends*. New York: HarperCollins, 1974.

Where the Sidewalk Ends

Garbage Poem

"Sarah Cynthia Sylvia Stout Would Not Take the Garbage Out" is a poem that describes the garbage that collects in Cynthia's house. Students can add lines to the poem by describing garbage using rhymes like Shel Silverstein. Students can make an illustration of their garbage.

Supplies

Practice paper

Drawing paper

Pencil

Instructions

1. Ask the students to write several lines to go with the poem.

2. Students can draw a picture to go along with the poem.

Silverstein, Shel. *Where the Sidewalk Ends*. New York: HarperCollins, 1974.

Whoever You Are

Carved Plaster

The frames around the illustrations are hand carved from plaster and wood with faux gems. Students can carve a design into a piece of drywall plaster.

Supplies

See the supply list on page 25 for drywall relief sculpture.

Pencil

Faux gems

Glue

Acrylic paint

Instructions

1. Follow the instructions on page 25 for carving the drywall.

2. Paint the finished design and glue on the faux gems.

Fox, Mem. *Whoever You Are*. Illustrated by Leslie Staub. San Diego: Harcourt Brace, 1997.

Mem Fox Website. URL: http://www.memfox.net/ (Accessed March 26, 2002).

Wool Gathering:
A Sheep Family Reunion

My Family Album

Family members are described in this book with poems and drawings. Students can make a photo album with drawings and poems about their family.

Supplies

See accordion book supplies on page 6

Squares of paper

Glue

Pencil

Practice writing paper

Instructions

1. Follow the instructions for an accordion book on page 6.

2. Have the students draw pictures of their family members on the small squares of paper.

3. Next, glue the picture in the accordion photo album. Students can use the practice paper to write poems that describe each person. Write the short poems under the pictures.

Wheeler, Lisa. *Wool Gathering: A Sheep Family Reunion.* Illustrated by Frank Ansley. New York: Atheneum Books for Young Readers, 2001.

Lisa Wheeler Website. URL: http://www.lisawheelerbooks.com/ (Accessed March 26, 2002).

Index

About the Author

Debi Englebaugh received a bachelor of fine arts degree in drawing from The Pennsylvania State University, certification in art education and a master of arts in fibers from Edinboro University of Pennsylvania. Debi lives in Hermitage, Pennsylvania, with her husband Robert and her two sons, Taylor and Morgan. She retired from teaching art after ten years to raise her sons. She is involved in the children's activities and well as volunteering in her community. Debi is a studio artist and currently works in the paper arts.